W9-BLY-889

Drawing on the latest research and theory and featuring candid in-person interviews, this book provides a map for the multiple pathways for negotiating a meaningful and rejuvenating second half of life. Nancy Schlossberg's planning matrices enable readers to integrate their personal psychological profile with future planning goals related to expectations concerning new or continuing work, relationships, sense of purpose, identity and health. The author is no mere cheerleader for some sentimentalized "golden years." She is an astute observer of both the vistas and roadblocks that each person making retirement-related decisions must face. Her own journey has taught her much. Now she's showing us the way ahead.

—*Ronald J. Manheimer, PhD, Executive Director,*
  North Carolina Center for Creative Retirement and
  Research Associate Professor of Philosophy,
  University of North Carolina at Asheville

Nancy Schlossberg is one of America's most thoughtful chroniclers of the changing nature of retirement and an invaluable guide to making the most of the period stretching beyond the middle years. *Revitalizing Retirement: Reshaping Your Identity, Relationships, and Purpose* is a wonderful book, packed with essential insights, compelling stories, and a road map to genuine fulfillment. It is essential reading!

—*Marc Freedman, PhD, Author,* Encore: Finding
  Work That Matters in the Second Half of Life

Revitalizing Retirement: Reshaping Your Identity, Relationships, and Purpose by retirement expert Dr. Nancy Schlossberg is insightful, accessible, and highly useful for the public, professionals, and program planners alike. Concepts like the Psychological Portfolio, reflecting a depth of understanding and wisdom, take you on a positive journey in relation to personal identity, purpose, and relationships. This book is not about making the best of, but creating the best in, retirement.

—*Gene D. Cohen, MD, PhD, Director,*
  Center on Aging, Health & Humanities,
  The George Washington University, Washington, DC

Revitalizing Retirement

Revitalizing Retirement

Reshaping Your Identity, Relationships, and Purpose

NANCY K. SCHLOSSBERG, EdD

American Psychological Association
Washington, DC

Second Printing December, 2010

Published by
American Psychological Association
750 First Street, NE
Washington, DC 20002
www.apa.org

To order
APA Order Department
P.O. Box 92984
Washington, DC 20090-2984
Tel: (800) 374-2721; Direct: (202) 336-5510
Fax: (202) 336-5502; TDD/TTY: (202) 336-6123
Online: www.apa.org/books/
E-mail: order@apa.org

In the U.K., Europe, Africa, and the Middle East, copies may be ordered from
American Psychological Association
3 Henrietta Street
Covent Garden, London
WC2E 8LU England

Typeset in Goudy and Minion by Circle Graphics, Inc., Columbia, MD

Printer: Sheridan Books, Ann Arbor, MI
Cover Designer: Naylor Design, Washington, DC
Technical/Production Editor: Harriet Kaplan

The opinions and statements published are the responsibility of the authors, and
such opinions and statements do not necessarily represent the policies of the
American Psychological Association.

Library of Congress Cataloging-in-Publication Data
Schlossberg, Nancy K., 1929-
  Revitalizing retirement : reshaping your identity, relationships, and purpose /
Nancy K. Schlossberg. — 1st ed.
      p. cm.
  Includes bibliographical references and index.
  ISBN-13: 978-1-4338-0413-7
  ISBN-10: 1-4338-0413-1
1. Retirement—Psychological aspects. 2. Retirement—Planning. I. Title.

HQ1062.S328 2009
646.7'9—dc22

                                    2008033094

British Library Cataloguing-in-Publication Data
A CIP record is available from the British Library.

Printed in the United States of America
First Edition

Laughter, simplicity and optimism have their place in . . . a complex and challenging world. And whether you live in a trailer or a penthouse, life does not seem to offer too many concrete answers. But it's nice to catch an occasional glimpse of truth and try to reflect it back, and if we're lucky, we might all share a moment of light.

—Robert Fulghum, *All I Really Need to Know I Learned in Kindergarten*

To Steve Schlossberg, the one and only; to Janet McKee, who introduced me to Steve and who has been my rock of Gibraltar; and to the late distinguished professor Morris Rosenberg, whose seminal work on mattering inspired my work and this book.

Contents

Acknowledgments

I am especially grateful to Lansing Hays, formerly at the American Psychological Association (APA), and Julia Frank McNeil, senior director of APA books, who convinced me to write a companion book to *Retire Smart, Retire Happy: Finding Your True Path in Life*. I am also grateful to other APA staff members who helped turn this book into a reality, especially Maureen Adams, Genevieve Gill, Harriet Kaplan, and Caryn McCleskey.

Friends and colleagues Willa and Bob Bernhard, Jan Birk, Janet Duke, Barbara Finkelstein, Carol Green, Jeanne Hansel, Johnette Isham, Allen Ivey, Stephanie Kay, Mickey and Bob Knox, Gail and Richard Levin, Norma Sue Madden, Molly McCartney, Janet McKee, Beryl Radin, Susan Robinson, Aina and Norman Segal, Ruth Lee and Rabbi Harold Silver, Sue Smock, and Mildred Wurf listened to me endlessly groan over writing a second book on retirement. Tim Dutton and Suzanne Gregory of SCOPE believed in my work on mattering and made me feel appreciated, noticed, and depended on.

There were many who helped formulate what needs to go into a book on retirement. Edith Fierst and Betsy Stephens, leaders of the Retirement Seminar Group, invited me to join their monthly luncheons as they discussed the ups and downs following retirement. Thanks also to Joan Aron, Nedra Hartzel, Linda Mendelsohn, and Steven Ebbin, who organized focus groups with retirees and perspective retirees; to Bob Riessett, Paul Recer, and Jim Harding, who participated in one of the focus groups; to the many men and women who shared their stories with me in individual interviews or as part of a focus group; and to Mark Savickes, who graciously analyzed a case from the narrative perspective.

Several scholars in the field of adult development and aging graciously sent me their papers and/or talked with me about their work, including Carmi Schooler of the National Institutes of Health; Dan P. McAdams of Northwestern University; and Paul Costa, codirector of the Baltimore Longitudinal Study of Aging.

Ellen Hoffman, an author of books on the financial aspects of retirement, edited the first draft of the book. I also had the help of editor Esther Gordon, who read the manuscript and offered invaluable comments. Betty Bowers, who typed the final draft, has seen me through every book with her patience and good spirit. In addition, I am fortunate to have a computer guru, Daniel Gormley Jr., always helpful, always there. I also thank Florence Rosenberg, widow of Morris Rosenberg and scholar in her own right, for her encouragement.

And special thanks to Michele and Mark Schlossberg, whose marriage brought such joy to our family, as well as Karen, Larry, and their children—my grandchildren—Robin and Jenny, who gave new meaning to the joys of getting older.

Last, but not least, I thank Darcy Corcoran, TV producer, who believed in my work and produced a PBS Pledge Special, *Retire Smart, Retire Happy,* which gave me a platform and introduced me to the ways of national television. What a happy time we had!

Revitalizing Retirement

Introduction

To my surprise, I recently discovered that writing this book really began in 1963, when I was working in the counseling center at Howard University in Washington, DC! Some long-lost notes for a lecture I gave then to freshmen had a familiar ring. I was urging them to follow their passion; to become involved; to be open to new experiences; and to know that they would continue growing, developing, and exploring. I talked about the issues that would concern them throughout their lives: their continual quest for identity, their questions about their competence to deal with life's challenges, and their search for the meaning of life. I talked around some issues for which there were no labels—their need to matter and the importance of attending to today while always looking ahead to tomorrow. As I discuss later in this chapter, I have come to recognize that these issues are central to people's ability to be psychologically healthy later in life as they make the transition from work to retirement.

After Howard University, I joined the faculty of Wayne State University in Detroit, Michigan. It was there that my fascination with adult development and aging began. My first study looked at men over 35 who had enrolled as undergraduates at Wayne State. They were, for the most part, blue-collar workers who wanted to improve their lives and were making changes despite social constraints. At the time of my study it was rare for adults to return to school. My aim was to study their motivations and experiences, but the study raised more questions than answers, chief among them being, were these men really changing?

After moving to the University of Maryland at College Park, where I spent the bulk of my career, I began my studies of adults in transition. I was intrigued by several questions: What makes it possible for a person to cope easily with one transition and then experience difficulty at another time? Are there any ways to help people cope more creatively? To answer those questions, I studied all kinds of transitions, including geographic moves, return to school, loss of one's job, divorce, and even transitions that did not occur when expected. At the end of each study, I would proclaim, "This is my last transition study." But somehow, I could not stop. My fascination with transitions continued and continues.

These studies challenged popular assumptions about age. I, like many others, felt I knew something about a person if I knew the person's age. The reality is that if you tell me someone is 60, I know nothing about that person. If you tell me that a particular 60-year-old is newly married, another 60-year-old has recently become unemployed, and yet another 60-year-old has been diagnosed with a critical illness, then I begin to know something about the possible joys and terrors the person is facing. My friend Norman, who celebrated his 90th birthday and passed his real estate exam the same week, clearly challenges any assumptions one might have about age and retirement. My conclusion is that the transitions you are experiencing in life tell more about you than your chronological age.

That leads to my studies of retirement. Although I realize now they were really a continuation of my work over the past 30 years, it was only when I faced my own retirement that I began to experience firsthand a transition that a burgeoning number of Americans will be navigating in the next decade or two. Retirement for me, initially, meant leaving my job as a tenured professor of counseling psychology at the University of Maryland, and—like so many others of my generation—moving to Florida with my husband. But these steps unleashed a series of unexpected challenges and questions about my place in the world and a sense that I'd lost my bearings as my connections with people and activities I'd depended on for decades to enrich my life were interrupted.

The more I focused and struggled to define my own retirement, looking through both my personal and professional lenses, the more I realized that we are living in a period when the very definition of the word *retirement* is changing. In the past, retirement simply meant that you no longer went to work every day. Because people lived fewer years than they do now, retirees didn't feel the need to embark on new, long-term projects or commitments. Retirement meant the rocking chair; spending time with the grandchildren; and, if your income permitted it, perhaps a nice vacation once a year.

WHAT'S RETIREMENT, ANYWAY?

Today, it's no longer clear what constitutes retirement. Susan P. Robinson, vice president of the Center for Life Long Learning, and Mary Beth Lakin, associate director for special projects at the American Council on Education, are engaged in a 2-year research project funded by the MetLife Foundation. In their initial report, they concluded that not only is retirement changing but so is the language used to describe it. "*Retirees* and *seniors* are now *rebounders, prime timers,* or *recareerers.* In short, the term *retirement* is being retired, or at least redefined. Instead, increasing numbers of adults aged 55 to 79 are entering the *third age* of life."[1]

It's tempting, but not accurate, to equate retirement with aging. For people in some fields—pilots, professional athletes, dancers, or people in the military—retirement comes at an early age. For them, retirement may imply entering a whole new career or starting a new business. Even for many people who are older, retirement may mean leaving a job but continuing to work, perhaps part time, perhaps on a different schedule or in a different field, whether for financial or other reasons. Simply knowing that someone is retired does not tell you much. You also need to know whether the person is continuing to work, changing course dramatically, moving into a life of leisure and fun, searching for the right niche, or perhaps still being involved but more as spectator than participant.

Writers and researchers have suggested that retirement is best understood as a series of stages rather than a single stage of life. For example, deputy editor Matthew Heimer and reporter Kristen Bellstrom wrote an extensive article on retirement for *SmartMoney* describing three distinct stages following retirement: "retiring to work," which could include a new part-time job, a phased retirement, or a return to school; entering the "wonder years" of travel and leisure; and "watching the sunset," which involves decisions about where to live and whether to move to a retirement or continuing care community.[2]

Similarly, a researcher on aging, psychiatrist Gene Cohen, identified adult developmental phases. He purposely used the term *phase* rather than *stage*, suggesting a more fluid process. After interviewing hundreds of people, he concluded that throughout life, people continue to grow "because of aging, not despite aging."[3] His theory of adult growth and development provides a new way to look at retirement and aging.

Cohen cited studies demonstrating that neurological changes in the brain enable adults to become more complex and creative—our bonus as we age.

This observation, combined with what he labeled *the inner push*, led him to identify four distinct developmental phases in the adult years:

1. *midlife reevaluation*, which is a better way to describe this "time for exploration and transition" than the term *midlife crisis;*
2. *liberation*, a "time to experiment";
3. *summing up*, a period to review one's life, followed by giving back through such activities as volunteering; and
4. *encore*, which he described as "the desire to go on, even in the face of adversity or loss."[4]

Cohen's encouraging research demonstrates that people continue to develop, but not in a lockstep, linear fashion.

Marc Freedman, author and founder of the Civic Engagement movement, described retirement as an "interlude between stages . . . [because] more and more individuals are 'retiring' for a period—to catch their breath—before making the transition to a new chapter in life."[5] I think of retirement as the bridge between leaving one set of roles, relationships, routines, and assumptions and developing a new set. It is a time to think about crafting a new life for yourself—whether it is playing golf, changing the world, caring for grandchildren or other family members, starting a new and different career, relaxing, volunteering, or studying. In other words, retirement does not mean that you will be doing a fixed set of activities—it is a transition to what's next.

At times, you might still be vitally engaged in work; at other times, you might be involved in reviewing your life and writing your memoir; at other times, you will adventure travel; and then you might find the need for an ongoing commitment and return to work. What becomes evident is that retirees have many options—that retirement does not mean the end, but rather the beginning of what some refer to as the *third age*.

The average 65-year-old woman today has a future life expectancy of more than 18 years and a man of the same age, 16 years. Yet many of us are unprepared and even confused about how to make the most of this gift—these "extra" years. When the market research firm Mintel conducted a survey of recent retirees, they found that 62% of those interviewed had retired without any idea of how they would craft a life or adjust to retirement.[6] In fact, sociologist Phyllis Moen was quoted as suggesting that people spend more time planning a wedding than planning for retirement.[7]

BOOMER DIVERSITY

The enormous number of baby boomers retiring, and their need for guidance, made me realize that there was a need for a different kind of book on retirement. The first baby boomer to sign up for Social Security, Kathleen Casey-Kirschling, was born on January 1, 1946, the beginning of the baby boomer tsunami. Thus, the first wave of 3.2 million baby boomers turned 62 in 2008. If Mintel's finding is correct, hundreds of thousands of adults every year will retire and feel at sea, wondering what to do and how to get a life for the next 20 or 30 years.[8]

It's often said that the surge of baby boomers will change the nature of retirement, implying that this is a monolithic group, but the fact is that the most outstanding characteristic of the boomers is their diversity. For example, *Baltimore Sun* reporter Linell Smith pointed to some perplexing facts: Many boomers are exercising and working out, yet 40% of boomer women are obese, and many boomers have considerable disposable income for travel and entertainment, but a quarter of them earn less than $35,000 a year.[9] With such diversity, of course, the boomers will follow different paths to and in retirement.

The following people, whom I interviewed during my research, exemplify this diversity:

- Teresa, 64, a lawyer and former human resource specialist in a government agency, and her 60-year-old husband, a labor negotiator, are retiring to two new homes—a house in Arizona and a condo at a beach resort.
- Wally interrupted his career as an interior designer to move back to Iowa City to care for his aging father. He was caught in a dilemma: too young to retire at age 56 but unwilling to let his father fend for himself.
- Ann, at 60, is starting a career as a psychotherapist after enrolling in a PhD program at age 50.

- Larry, a 50-year-old house painter with a bad back, no pension, and little savings, is still working. He is trying to figure out how he can retire and care for his health.

According to author and sociologist Lillian Rubin, "Clearly, there is no template for our futures" as individual boomers or even preboomers retire and age.[10] However, living long enough to face the challenge of figuring out "what's next" can provide us with an opportunity to live out some dreams that we were not able to realize earlier. The one thing that seems certain, as we tend to live longer, is that most of us will always be leaving one path and starting out on another. It will be up to each of us to carve out a life that continues to have meaning and excitement, a life that makes us feel we are still important but in different ways than before.

THIS BOOK'S CENTERPIECE—MATTERING

A few years ago, I wrote and published *Retire Smart, Retire Happy: Finding Your True Path in Life*.[11] After its publication, I continued to collect stories about what makes a successful or happy retirement. These new stories were so compelling that I decided to share what I had learned in a new, companion book. During this time, an interviewer asked me, "Have you found any surprises as you interviewed men and women for your new book?" My answer was yes: Whether I was speaking to men or women, rich or poor, young or old, all expressed a common theme and challenge—the need to be noticed and to feel important, sought after, appreciated, and depended on by others.

The late distinguished sociologist from the University of Maryland, Morris Rosenberg, coined the term *mattering* to describe these needs. Rosenberg identified mattering as an overlooked motive—one that explains performance, behavior, even well-being. He pointed out how critical it is to believe that we are important to others, often in their thoughts, and that our lives make a difference to them. Mattering to oneself, to others, and to the world is the coordinating, although not single, issue that guides our understanding of ourselves. In assessing whether we matter, we first ask ourselves, "Do I know who I am? Do I appreciate myself? Do I feel competent?" Then we ask, "Are my inside and outside worlds congruent? Do others appreciate me? Do my work and community worlds make me feel needed?"[12]

Let me explain how I became interested in the concept of mattering. I read a book chapter by Rosenberg and McCullough that analyzed studies about adolescent boys and delinquency and concluded that those who felt they mattered to parents, teachers, and school engaged in less delinquent behavior than those who felt that no one cared about them or depended on them. At the end of the chapter, Rosenberg and McCullough included a surprise observation that had nothing to do with adolescent boys:

> It has been suggested that one problem of retirement is that one no longer matters; others no longer depend upon us. . . . The reward of retirement, involving a

surcease from labor, can be the punishment of not mattering. Existence loses its point and savor when one no longer makes a difference.[13]

Rosenberg's concept of mattering is a universal, lifelong issue that connects us all. Think of Willy Loman, the protagonist in Arthur Miller's play *Death of a Salesman*. Rosenberg described Loman's desire

to excel, to win out over anonymity and meaningless-ness, to love and . . . be loved, and above all . . . to *count*. When he roared out, "I am not a dime a dozen! I am Willy Loman . . ." he was expressing this desperate need for significance.[14]

I found myself using Rosenberg's ideas in subsequent work. A book I coauthored, *Improving Higher Education Environments for Adults: Responsive Programs and Services From Entry to Departure*, described the degree to which postsecondary environments were responsive to the needs of adult learners.[15] Actually, we were studying the degree to which adult learners felt they mattered, and we found a relationship between retention and the degree to which they felt they mattered. For example, Melinda, considered a star student, dropped out of the university. Why? Because she felt pulled in all directions—trying to help her children as a single parent, holding down a part-time job, traveling to the university for her classes. Moreover, there was no place to relax and interact with other adult learners; she felt isolated. In other words, there was no institutional support for her. A simple so-lution would have been an adult learner lounge, but sufficient space was unavailable. Eventually, she saw no reason to stay. She is now a real estate agent and has not completed the degree she had wanted. She did not feel she mattered to the institution.

In the present volume, I draw on Rosenberg's work on mattering and describe how it relates to retirement. His death and the loss of his unfinished manuscript on mattering leave a hole in our understanding of the concept and its implications, but we are fortunate to have one of his unpublished chapters. His work influenced two important studies by his wife, Florence Rosenberg—one of Army wives and one of widows—demonstrating that those Army wives and widows who feel they still matter may find it easier to cope with other problems and to reconstruct their lives.[16, 17]

Mattering is crucial to our well-being, and we all need to figure out ways to bolster our own sense that we count. The next section defines and examines the different strategies you can use to make sure you feel that you matter.

YOUR PSYCHOLOGICAL PORTFOLIO

Most of us have ways of checking up on how we're doing in life. For example, we track our financial portfolios. We receive monthly financial statements, agonize over them, modify them, and change financial advisers if we're displeased. Financial planners usually take a long-range view and warn against proclaiming a catastrophe if the bottom line is not what you want it to be this month. When your personal situation changes, you and your financial planner, advisor, or accountant will rebalance your portfolio, making the best allocations among various types of investments. Many retirement books emphasize how to manage your finances so that you can both enjoy retirement and pay your bills. They walk readers through the elements of a financial portfolio, suggesting what types of assets are appropriate, how to balance them, and how to generate the return needed to enjoy retirement life. That is clearly important.

Similarly, many of us go to the doctor for a yearly physical checkup. The doctor checks our weight, questions us about our smoking and exercising, and recommends lab tests to monitor how we're doing physically. If the doctor suggests a different diet or pill or gives us a talking-to about getting exercise, we feel as if we've done something positive to maintain our health.

Now I'm going to suggest that you add regular checkups of your psychological resources. Few of us even realize we have what I now call a *Psychological Portfolio*. Yet we all have a set of psychological resources that can help us negotiate any major transition—and retirement is certainly major.

Although I touched on many such resources, including identity, relationships, and paths, in my earlier retirement book, only recently have I begun to see them as part and parcel of your Psychological Portfolio. Retirement challenges your Identity, changes your Relationships, and may leave you feeling rootless if you have no Purpose. These three components—Identity,

Relationships, and Purpose—make up each person's Psychological Portfolio and are the focus of this book.

WHAT'S IN THIS BOOK?

The goal of this book is to describe the psychological skills and tools you can use to identify and meet the challenges you'll face in your next phase of life—whether that phase includes traditional retirement or a brand-new path you'll create for yourself. My previous book made the case for acknowledging the emotional side of the transition from full-time work to full or partial retirement. This book extends that to focus on how you can strengthen yourself by considering mattering as the bottom-line issue. Ask yourself, "Does this path, activity, or vision make me feel worthwhile? Am I following the path that makes sense for me?" This book articulates more sharply what you need to be happy, the importance of feeling that you matter in retirement, and strategies for getting there.

Just so you know what is not in this book: I do not cover ways to solidify your financial portfolio, nor do I cover in detail other important aspects of life, such as developing and maintaining a healthy body through exercise, nutrition, and spirituality. They are critical elements of a happy retirement; however, the book cannot cover everything. I therefore made the decision to stay focused on two main issues: paying attention to your need to matter and strengthening your Psychological Portfolio. Of course, it is impossible to neatly separate life into component parts. When I conduct workshops, I prefer to collaborate with financial planners and health care professionals to show the importance of integrating finances, wellness, and psychological resources in planning for retirement. This book covers material that will provide another dimension for financial planners, wellness experts, physical therapists, psychologists, social workers, and trainers to use in their work with retirees.

Part I, "The Key to a Happy Retirement," deals with what you need in retirement. Chapter 1, "Mattering and Happiness in Retirement," defines mattering and happiness, showing how the two concepts go together. Chapter 2, "Check Your Psychological Portfolio," covers the three elements—Identity, Relationships, and Purpose—that lead to retirement happiness if you consciously work on maintaining and strengthening them.

Part II, "How Others Have Found Happiness" (chaps. 3, 4, and 5), recounts stories of people who have aced retirement by using creative strategies. These stories, as well as tips on reshaping the elements of your Psychological Portfolio, will guide you as you navigate what's next.

You will find ways to improvise your own journey to happiness in Part III, "Creating Your Own Happiness." But your journey cannot begin until you face the internal and external roadblocks that could push you off track. After addressing these roadblocks in chapter 6, "It's About You: Design Your Own Psychological Portfolio," you will start establishing a new structure and making your own chart for the future. Chapter 7, "Three Guidelines for a Better Retirement," frames retirement as a transition filled with surprises. Your success will depend on learning how to apply wisdom to your choices. Chapter 8, "Create a Lifetime of Possibilities," revisits the importance of making happiness and mattering your priority, with lifelong learning a major means of accomplishing that. I end with a short Afterword.

The story line is straightforward: If you feel that you are appreciated and that you matter, you have the potential for a happy retirement. But happiness does not grow on trees. You have to be intentional about making it happen. As you look at how others have strengthened their Identity, Relationships, and Purpose, you will see ways to make retirement the time of your life.

At the end of each chapter, there is a section called "It's Your Turn." These sections include tips and questions, like a friendly hand that will help you see the implications of what you have just read for your own life. For example, in chapter 3, on Identity, I ask you to think about ways to make yourself feel you matter. I also suggest that you question others about how they have reshaped their identities in retirement. In other words, "It's Your Turn" suggests activities for you to apply to your own life.

A WORD ABOUT SOURCES

I have studied the literature on retirement, aging, and midlife from the perspective of individuals considering retirement or already retired. Subsequently, as I wrote,

I checked some of the assertions I made with those who have studied the subject academically. Citations from the literature are provided in the Notes at the end of the book.

To gather material for this book, I met with several groups of retirees. Some were ongoing groups, and others were created specifically to discuss the issues addressed here.

Ongoing groups included Retired Old Men Eating Out (ROMEO), a group of psychologists in Sarasota, Florida, led by Allen Ivey; the Same Boat Group of retired men and women in Washington, DC, led by Joan Aron and Steven Ebbin; the Retirement Seminar Group in Washington, DC, led by Edith Fierst and Betsy Stephens; the Baby Boomer Party Group in Sarasota, Florida, led by Johnette Isham; and the groups of retired men and retired baby boomers organized by TV producer Darcy Corcoran for the PBS special, *Retire Smart, Retire Happy*.

I asked professionals in several organizations to convene focus groups of retirees. I met with the University of Maryland's volunteer group, led by Linda Mendelsohn; a group of State Department retirees, led by Nedra Hartzel; and a group of retired police, organized by Timothy Scott of the International Union of Police Associations.

SCOPE, a community organization in Sarasota, Florida, surveyed 35 members of a neighborhood association with questions to ascertain if they felt they mattered and, if so, how. In addition, I interviewed

25 individuals in depth and another 25 in casual conversation and by e-mail.

With these individuals' privacy in mind, I have used pseudonyms and disguised cities and occupations. When I use both first and last names, they are actual names of people I interviewed, and they have given me permission to use their stories in this book.

CONCLUSION

Leading a successful retirement is about much more than money. It's about feeling you matter, that you are and will be noticed and appreciated. You can make this happen by finding ways to enhance your Identity, your Relationships, and your Purpose in life. Read on!

IT'S YOUR TURN: SOME QUESTIONS TO CONSIDER

1. How do you define retirement?
2. What is your reaction to applying the word *retiree* to yourself?
3. Think about the two main concepts described in this chapter—mattering and the Psychological Portfolio. As you read the book, your ideas about both may change.

I

THE KEY TO A HAPPY RETIREMENT

1

Mattering and Happiness in Retirement

I was giving a speech about ways to prepare for retirement when a woman in the audience questioned me. "You have presented the challenges that accompany the retirement transition," she said, "but you have left out the most important challenge—the importance of finding happiness and inner peace."

As I thought about her comment, I realized that I had missed the boat. I had been talking about decision-making strategies—how to know if you are ready to retire, how to decide which path to follow in retirement, and how to make sure you are aware of what is at stake when you retire. But this approach did not take into account an underlying concern: Will I be happy? Will I still matter?

I interviewed Jules, a policeman from Washington, DC, who illustrates this point. Deflated when he retired from his demanding but rewarding career, he told me, "I turned in my gun and badge, and that was that." The department had done nothing to prepare him psychologically for retirement. After moving to another state, he took a few part-time jobs, but nothing clicked. The work was fairly menial and made him even more aware of what he had left behind. The abruptness of the transition made him angry, and with no other place to focus his anger, he turned it inward and became depressed.

Jules kept in touch by e-mail with his former brother-in-law, Jim, who managed an exclusive resort. When his assistant manager suddenly left, Jim contacted Jules immediately and begged him to fill in as a stopgap measure. Jules and his wife moved, and that fill-in job has lasted 8 years. Jules credits the invitation to work in a responsible job with saving his life. It was not the content of the job that saved his life; it was that once again, like Humpty Dumpty, he was back together again. He once again feels he matters and is happy with his life.

When talking with those in transition—a recent widow, an Army wife, an adolescent boy, an adult learner, a retiree, or an unemployed person—the conversation often turns to the need to belong, to matter.

MATTERING: A UNIVERSAL NEED

As I discussed in the Introduction, sociologist Morris Rosenberg coined the concept of *mattering*—the need to feel noticed, appreciated, and depended on—to describe a universal, and often overlooked, motive that influences our thinking and behavior. In other words, it is important for people to believe that they count in others' lives and that they make a difference to them. Rosenberg also suggested, and I have found, that retirees who no longer feel appreciated can experience retirement as "perplexing."[1]

Five Dimensions of Mattering

Rosenberg and his students were studying mattering in general. I decided it would be informative to test his theory on a specific population—adult learners in postsecondary institutions. Anne Lassalle, Renee Golec, and I found that if the policies, practices, and classroom activities of an institution were geared toward making adult learners feel they mattered, these learners would remain in school and complete their program of study. As part of the study, we developed the Mattering Scale based on Rosenberg's five dimensions of mattering.[2]

1. Attention

According to Rosenberg and McCullough, "The most elementary form of mattering is the feeling that one commands interest or notice of another person."[3] When sociology professor emeritus Robert S. Weiss retired, he commented, "I still have an office . . . and it is the smallest office I have occupied since leaving my graduate student cubicle. . . . When I attend a professional conference . . . I tend to feel marginal."[4] One adult learner felt she was irrelevant to the university where she was studying because offices closed at 4:30, and advisers were rarely available. A postal employee quit her job when she realized she was never going to be promoted, even though she had participated in voluntary training.

2. Importance

Importance can be defined as being the object of another person's concern and belief that he or she cares about what we want, think, and do. *New York Times* columnist David Brooks described the need for importance as follows: "Let me tell you what men want . . . recognition. Men want others to recognize their significance. They want to feel important and part of something important."[5]

3. Appreciation

When we feel appreciated, we feel that others are thankful for who we are and what we do. One woman reported, "I spend hours volunteering, but it is worth it; the members of the organization let me know how much my work means to them."

4. Dependence

All of us depend on others, but what is special about mattering is that it focuses on others' dependence on us. As one man reported, "Even though my wife died recently, my work team depends on my being there. If it were not for that, I would stay home and just cry."

5. Pride

Another element of mattering is when we feel that others will feel proud of us—be glad about our accomplishments—and disappointed for us if we fail. I interviewed Malcolm, who told me, "I am 65 and just completed my BA degree. I had been a maintenance worker in the school system and always dreamed about completing my BA. My family, especially my adult children, were so excited at the graduation ceremony and are so proud of me."

Four Contexts of Mattering

The retirement transition brings the issue of mattering into clear focus. In many cases, the huge role that work played in our daily life becomes clear only after retirement. "Working" and "going to work" imply much more than just doing a job. The loss of the substance and challenge of the work itself, our relationships with colleagues, the connection to a physical environment, an office to go to, and the daily routines can leave a gaping hole, causing people to wonder, with so much newfound spare time, whether they matter any more.

But these losses do not have to be permanent. I have found that retirees can replace these connections in many ways, such as by (a) taking on new activities that are similar to work life, (b) contributing to their community, (c) creating new relationships with friends or family, and (d) finding ways to matter to themselves.

Mattering Through Work

When we talk about the relationship between mattering and retirement, we're often focusing on the degree to which work contributes to our sense of mattering. One way to replace the sense of mattering one loses by retiring is to engage in some other type of work, whether paid or volunteer.

A case in point is Lenny, a former employee of a large nonprofit organization, who expected to be treated as a senior statesman after his voluntary retirement. But following retirement, he no longer felt important. For 2 years after his retirement, Lenny was in limbo, unsure of his identity, competence, and future. To complicate matters, he convinced his wife to move to a North Carolina golf community, which she hated.

> It was the first time we fought, and it took me a little time to turn things around. Since writing has always been therapeutic for me, I wrote about my experience in a book. As a result, I was invited to give seminars on retirement to several Fortune 100 companies.

He once again regained his sense of purpose.

One member of a focus group I conducted had been forced into early retirement. She told me,

> I felt unappreciated, thrown away. After a year and a half in forced retirement, my self-esteem went downhill. After 2 years of battling with the organization that eliminated me, I was given a part-time job as coordinator of a program that places volunteers in appropriate offices in the organization. I am beginning to feel as if I matter

again. The volunteers really appreciate what I am doing for them. I feel much better, but I still resent that I had to go through an ugly process to force myself back into the system. But I swallowed my pride, and I am glad I did it. Mattering really matters.

A former accountant, a member of another focus group, found satisfaction in volunteering. She began by doing a series of short-term volunteer assignments for a number of organizations, like ushering for the opera and assisting in a congressional office. Then she moved into a slot as a permanent volunteer for AARP with a regular schedule. Helping seniors fill out their income tax returns made her feel really appreciated and depended on in a different way than before.

Tali's story is an example of how one person created a new life where she felt, once again, that she mattered. In her mid-60s, she voluntarily retired from her job as dean of a business school in the Midwest. Her children were married, she was divorced, and she had wanted for a long time to try something new. Ignoring the warnings of her friends, she moved to Washington, DC, realizing "it was now or never." Before becoming a dean, Tali had been in charge of a research center that depended on grants for its survival. When she arrived in Washington, she contacted the executive director of a nonprofit organization with whom she had served on a board and offered to write grant proposals for him on an ad hoc basis. After a few months, she became a senior consultant, with an office and a regular schedule.

After getting settled in her new apartment, she also began to volunteer at a political club. Within several years, she had taken on a leadership role in a major project for the club—strategic planning. These activities provided a social life for her while also allowing her to make substantive contributions to the organization's programs and goals.

Tali is a good illustration of Rosenberg's definition of the basic dimensions of mattering. She felt that she was receiving the *attention* she wanted; that she was *important* to others and that they cared about what she wanted, thought, and did; that she was *appreciated* for what she did; and that others *depended* on her. Because of her consulting job, Tali had a place to go, a place where she belonged.

At one point, Tali fell and broke her leg, and for some time she was forced to cut back on her work. Right before her surgery, she called her office, and 5 days after the surgery, she was back on the phone and computer, despite her pain. Her feeling that both groups depended on her motivated her to get well and keep working.

Tali took a big risk by leaving her job as a dean and her friends, sister, married children, and three grandchildren by moving to a new city. But the risk paid off. She has orchestrated a new life in which she feels she matters.

Mattering to the Community

Finding a way to matter to your community can also contribute to a higher quality of life for retirees. Robert

D. Putnam, Harvard professor and author, used the metaphor of bowling alone to illustrate the degree to which Americans are disconnected from each other. He developed ways to assess the degree of connectedness in any community and described new approaches and strategies that would engage people. In addition, he conducted nearly 500,000 interviews and discovered that people are less connected today than in earlier times. His conclusion was that connectedness through social networks improves mental health.[6]

Marc Freedman founded Civic Ventures to provide opportunities for older and retired people to regain a sense of purpose and feel part of a community. He encourages companies to open jobs to older workers and encourages individuals to engage in civic activities—a win–win situation. His work shows how engagement makes people feel good about themselves and believe that they matter.[7]

Freedman's work is being tested in Sarasota County, an area of Florida with many retirees. SCOPE, a community organization, has as its mission making Sarasota a city that will engage members of the community in discussions about ways to improve the quality of life for all its citizens. To accomplish that, SCOPE has initiated an aging project and invited all members of the community to participate in community conversations about ways to make Sarasota a truly intergenerational community. As a result of this initiative, the city was a finalist for an All-America City award, which is a program of the National Civic League (see http://www.ncl.org). The award honors cities that have pulled together government, business, and volunteer organizations to address and, it is hoped, solve local issues.

Tim Dutton, director of SCOPE, attributed the honor to the fact that SCOPE identified mattering as a key concept guiding the direction of SCOPE's involvement with the community. He wrote,

> We know how important it is for people who are aging to continue to believe that they "matter" . . . Mattering knows no age. It drives our decisions to vote, to engage in civic life, to be involved in our children's education, to mow a sick neighbor's lawn. What SCOPE contributes is a fledgling and sincere effort to increase the opportunities and ways each person can matter. . . . There is a connection between "mattering" and a vibrant, healthy, sustainable and equitable community.[8]

As part of SCOPE's initiative on aging, the organization conducted a neighborhood survey that included three questions on mattering. This survey was collected from 35 individuals, 20 of whom belonged to a neighborhood association and 15 of whom volunteered in a program that provided caregiver respite. The majority of these individuals were retired seniors.

The first question, "Where do you feel that your gifts are recognized and appreciated?", evoked many responses (respondents could answer more than once). Most of the respondents ranked family as the major source of appreciation (23), followed by neighborhood (17), and then place of worship (14). Place of employment received only 5 responses, and community only 1.

The responses to the second question, "Do people depend on you for these talents/gifts/skills?", showed that most respondents felt that others depended on them. Specifically, 21 answered "yes," 7 answered "somewhat," and 3 answered "no."

The third question, "What are some of the specific ways that make you feel appreciated?", confirmed what I have found from interviews. Most (28) found that "being called upon for help" made them feel they mattered. Thirteen said that "being invited to join an organization" made them feel they mattered, followed by 7 who answered that "being asked about my talents/skills/gifts" was important, and 1 each mentioning as important "being thanked for volunteering," "being appreciated for what you are doing," and "hugging."

These responses reflect two important ways to make people feel they matter—(a) extending the power of invitation and (b) asking about their skills. And when people feel they matter, they can improve their communities. For example, in activities facilitated by SCOPE, residents of several neighborhoods joined together to clean up the yards of those unable to do so themselves. In other places, caregivers were invited to come together to develop respite opportunities for themselves and their families. These stories, and many more, illustrate how important it was for these Sarasota residents to feel they mattered and to be part of making others feel they matter.

Mattering to Family and Friends

Human beings are complex, and their need to feel that they matter extends beyond the sphere of work. Rosenberg believed that

> interpersonal mattering—mattering to specific others—has the most powerful impact on the psychological well-being of most people. People may feel that they make little difference to the world at large, or even to some smaller institution, without experiencing much psychological distress. But to feel that they do not matter to other human beings—that can be devastating.[9]

What if you matter to your colleagues at work or in your volunteer job but feel unappreciated at home? I met with a group of National Football League players' wives to discuss how they handled their complex lives. One said,

> My husband has time for everyone but me and the children. Yet he gets angry when we don't cater to his beck and call. He says we don't appreciate his pressures. He is right. I am through appreciating him. I need him to appreciate me.

Later, I read in the newspaper that they had divorced. We all know how important it is to feel we matter to our friends and family. And when they make us feel irrelevant and unimportant, we pull away.

Mattering to Yourself

At the end of the day, you need to ask if you appreciate yourself regardless of what others think of you. If your sense of self depends solely on others' opinions of you, you might experience times when you feel sad or even depressed.

Assess Whether You Matter

You can apply the concept of mattering to yourself by analyzing the different components of your life. First, consider whether you matter on the five dimensions of mattering: attention, importance, appreciation, dependence, and pride.

Next, examine the four contexts of mattering. If you are still in the labor force—either as a part- or full-time paid worker or as a volunteer on a regular basis—examine how you matter through your work activities. Then assess the degree to which you matter to your community; to your family and friends; and, finally, to yourself. In other words, you matter in different ways in different aspects of your life. Exhibit 1.1 can help guide your analysis.

THE MATTERING RECIPE

I have been asked many times if there is a recipe to follow to make sure you matter. Although there are no exact measurements for success, there are four ingredients that can help to give a sense of mattering to your life. They are (a) getting involved and staying engaged, (b) harnessing the power of invitations, (c) taking initiative, and (d) doing your best to make others feel that they matter. This section discusses each of these ingredients in turn.

EXHIBIT 1.1. Mattering Worksheet

Answer yes or no to the statements below to indicate if you feel you matter in each area.

Statement	Do you feel you matter in this area?	
	Yes	No
Five points of mattering		
Attention: I have a place to go to where I am expected—for example, an office, a club, an organization, a coffee shop.		
Importance: I am active as a volunteer or worker, and I feel that others think what I do is important.		
Appreciation: I am pleased that what I am doing is appreciated by others.		
Dependence: My club, organization, workplace, or friends depend on my being there.		
Pride: I feel that others are proud of my accomplishments.		
Four contexts of mattering		
I matter at work.		
I matter in my community.		
I matter to my family and friends.		
I matter to myself.		

For each statement for which you marked "no," consider how you could make yourself matter more. For example, if you do not feel you are receiving the attention, importance, appreciation, dependence, or pride that you want, consider which parts of the mattering recipe you can put some effort into. By the same token, if you feel you do not matter at work, in your community, with family and friends, or with yourself, consider which parts of the mattering recipe you will use to matter more. Now, on a separate sheet of paper, write down two or three things you will start doing today to increase your number of "yes" responses.

Get Involved, Stay Engaged

Throughout the book, you will hear a message repeated: Engage in life. That message is more than rhetoric; it is based on evidence. Carmi Schooler, a researcher at the National Institute of Mental Health, and her colleague, Mulatu Mestin Samuel, studied the increase in intellectual functioning of older people participating in and exposed to challenging work and leisure activities, especially when these activities were "substantively complex," requiring self-direction and decision making. Playing bridge, writing a grant proposal, doing a crossword puzzle, and figuring out how to initiate a project are all examples of substantively complex activities. Their studies, one conducted in 1974 of 883 men and their wives engaged in work and the other in 1994 of 315 men and 320 women pursuing leisure activities, showed that with regard to intellectual functioning, the axiom "use it or lose it" holds true.[10]

How do we combat the fear expressed when people say, "I think I'm losing it"? Answer: *lifelong learning*, which is the continuous process of learning new skills and acquiring new knowledge in a variety of formal and informal settings all through life. The growth of such opportunities is mind-boggling. Elderhostel, the major educational and travel organization for adults over the age of 55, has grown from 220 programs offered in 1975 to well over 8,000 offerings, with more than 100,000 adults participating in more than 500 lifelong learning institutes throughout the country (see their Web site: http://www.elderhostel.org). In addition, there are

37

other learning opportunities available at community centers, senior centers, and postsecondary education institutions. Many reasons exist for this revolution. One man, active in the Institute for Lifelong Learning at the University of South Florida, explained, "I participate for intellectual stimulation, and being part of a community of like-minded individuals." Active engagement, whether or not it is part of lifelong education, provides the stimulation to continue to grow and develop well into old age.

Masterpiece Living, an experimental program that emerged from the MacArthur Foundations' 10-year study on successful aging, has been instituted in 14 continuing care communities designed to engage residents in intellectual, spiritual, and physical activities.[11] According to Robert L. Kahn, professor emeritus of psychology and public health at the University of Michigan, the experiment involves studying the degree to which lifestyle changes enhance residents' feelings of well-being. The point person in each facility is a *lifestyle coordinator*, whose job is to increase residents' physical and volunteer activities and coach them about successful aging. To determine the efficacy of this experiment, researchers, in partnership with the Mayo Clinic, tested individuals before the introduction of the program and a year later to assess improvements in medical risk factors like blood pressure, blood sugar, cholesterol, and weight. This experiment has been accumulating an enormous amount of data, proving the point that intentional engagement works.

Harness the Power of Invitation

As I mentioned earlier in this chapter, Tim Dutton of SCOPE often discusses the power of invitation. When Paul, one of the participants in a men's focus group, voluntarily retired from his role an investigative reporter, he felt a bit at loose ends. When he was recruited back to cover some seminal stories, he was delighted. Although he did not want to return to work except on an ad hoc basis, he felt he still counted. So take advantage of invitations and opportunities!

When Elsie, a casual acquaintance, left her job as librarian, she gave up her office. She tried going back a few times to see how things were going, but she realized that without an invitation, she was no longer welcome. She felt like an intruder. Many universities offer an invitation by making office space available to retired professors; law firms offer many retired senior partners an office and the title "Of Counsel." When retirees are invited back, it helps them gradually break past ties as they move on to something new.

Take Initiative

Be on the alert for opportunities that you can create yourself. For example, I received the following e-mail from a recent retiree:

> Essentially, I set up my entire retirement agenda through initial e-mail contacts with employees in a branch office in Tucson, Arizona, of the bank where I worked, some 6 to 9 months before my arrival there. Thus, all I had to

do was to contact these individuals to meet them face to face. And each of these contacts led to a second or third contact. One of the contacts suggested me as a volunteer to help out at a booth on Arts Day. This was an excellent way to make more contacts and feel useful. Another contact put me in charge of parking at a special evening function at my church, providing the opportunity for me to become acquainted with some key church members and staff.

Make Others Feel They Matter

One of my husband Steve's deputies, when he worked in the Department of Labor, prepared a superb memo. Steve complimented her on the memo and asked if others had helped in its preparation. The deputy acknowledged the contributions of several other staff members, so Steve suggested that she rewrite the memo crediting those who had contributed and send them copies. Steve's instruction here is the moral of the story: Always be on the alert for ways to make others feel they matter.

Also, look for ways to institutionalize mattering activities. For example, many corporations have discovered the obvious—that new employees at all levels feel marginal. They are not part of the system and do not know the norms or the informal rules of how to get along and get things done in the organization. The need to identify "socializing agents," experienced employees who can help them with this joining process, has worked wonders in some organizations such as

Corning Glass. Turnover has been reduced and morale heightened.

Even the board of a city club, whose president discussed the issue with me, realized the importance of making new members feel they matter. The club prided itself on its rigorous intellectual standards for admission. Presumably, everyone admitted had high achievements in a field and years of experience. Yet the board found that many new members did not participate in the life of the club. Why? After many discussions, they realized that new members, even those of national and international renown, often feel awkward when entering a new system, be it a job or a club. They do not feel welcome, nor do they know how to integrate themselves. The board established a new member orientation committee with the sole purpose of involving new members. The committee established many activities, including informal receptions, telephone calls encouraging attendance at functions, and introductions of new members to committees where there might be a meshing of interests. As one new member said, "This was an enormous help—I am shy in new situations."

The growth of "intentional communities" of likeminded individuals designed to meet the needs of older people exemplifies a small but growing trend in this country. These communities are designed to enhance the lives of their residents by stressing their interdependence. Journalist Barry Yeoman chronicled the ingenuity of a group of people as they designed and built a community around similar interests where there was mutual sharing and caring. He described the variety of such communities, ranging from those with a religious orientation to those organized around specific interests such as music or theater.[12]

Summing Up

There are many ways to create environments where people can join together for fun, protection, security, and intimacy. The main ingredient is your own involvement followed by taking initiative, intentionally making others feel they matter, and, by example, showing how they can bring others in. Now for a leap of faith: I believe that if you matter, you will be happy. Can I prove that? The answer is no. But my interviews have led me to conclude that mattering and happiness go hand in hand.

HAPPINESS: AN ELUSIVE CONCEPT

All of us feel entitled to happiness, and rightly so. After all, the U.S. Declaration of Independence clearly stated, "We hold these truths to be self-evident, that all men are created equal, that they are endowed by their Creator with certain unalienable Rights, that among these are Life, Liberty and the pursuit of Happiness."

But what is this thing called happiness? People are constantly trying to define it, but the definition is slippery. What's more, it is ever-changing. Even though happiness is a hot topic, with experts writing literally hundreds of articles and books and appearing on TV shows addressing the issue, the definition of what makes us happy is elusive. Is it fame, power, money? Is it marriage, children, friendship? Is it self-knowledge, mindfulness, contemplation? Is it a sunset, the birth of a baby, a butterfly emerging? Is it doing work you love, painting a picture, moving into your first apartment or house? Or is it all of the above? And will it be the same tomorrow—will your happiness last?

Happiness is now a legitimate avenue for academic study. More than 200 colleges and universities, including Harvard, offer courses in positive psychology with a focus on happiness. One of the Harvard psychologists studying happiness, Daniel Gilbert, has suggested that we think often about what will make us happy. In fact, "each of us is a part-time resident of tomorrow" because "12 percent of our daily thoughts are about the future. . . . We like to frolic in the best of all imaginary tomorrows."[13]

Positive psychologist Martin Seligman suggested that we all have an "emotional baseline—a level of happiness" to which we almost inevitably return. For example, you can feel on top of the world because of a really happy time, like a glorious wedding on the beach at sunset or a move into your dream house. After the euphoria dies down, you return to your emotional baseline or your "enduring level of happiness," which varies considerably from person to person.[14] This is reminiscent of the set point theory of weight loss: You might diet and lose weight often, but you tend to return to the same weight each time.[15]

The good news is that we can change our happiness level. According to Sonja Lyubomirsky, psychology professor and author of *The How of Happiness*, one's happiness level is determined by three things: 50% by one's emotional baseline, 10% by one's life circumstances, and 40% by "intentional activity." She coined the phrase *40 percent solution:* You can boost your happiness by 40% if you engage in intentional activities. Lyubomirsky developed her Subjective Happiness Scale to determine a baseline level of happiness; see Exhibit 1.2.[16]

EXHIBIT 1.2. Subjective Happiness Scale

For each of the following statements or questions, circle the number from the scale that you think is most appropriate in describing you.

In general, I consider myself:

Not a very happy person					A very happy person	
1	2	3	4	5	6	7

Compared with most of my peers, I consider myself:

Less happy					More happy	
1	2	3	4	5	6	7

Some people are generally very happy. They enjoy life regardless of what is going on, getting the most out of everything. To what extent does this characterization describe you?

Not at all					A great deal	
1	2	3	4	5	6	7

(continued)

EXHIBIT 1.2. Subjective Happiness Scale *(continued)*

Some people are generally not very happy. Although they are not depressed, they never seem as happy as they might be. To what extent does this characterization describe you?

Not at all   A great deal

| 1 | 2 | 3 | 4 | 5 | 6 | 7 |

How to calculate your happiness score:
Step 1: Calculate your total score.

Item 1: _____ + Item 2: _____ + Item 3: _____
+ Item 4: _____ = _____.

Step 2: Calculate your happiness score.

Total from above: _____ $\div$ 4 = _____.

If your score is greater than 5.6, then you're happier than the average person. If your happiness score is not where you want it, the question becomes, "What should I do about it?" Think of some times when you were happy. Then try to come up with some ways to make that happen again. Your answers to the questions are your indicators about what you have to do. This book offers many suggestions throughout to help you move in the direction you desire.

But we are still left with the question, "What is happiness?" Gilbert suggested that the answer to that question has "vexed scientists and philosophers for millennia" because the word is used in many different ways.[17] Let's look at different perspectives on understanding happiness.

Happiness, according to some, is the pursuit of a goal, or it can refer to living an engaged life with a purpose, or it can be the search to find inner peace, or it can be an emotional reaction. These approaches to happiness are not necessarily exclusive, and what makes you happy at one point in your life might be different at another time. Right now, I am happy to be engaged in writing this book—it provides a purpose. At times, I might be concentrating on my inner, spiritual life while sitting at the beach listening to the waves, and many times I have loved the process of reading a book or watching a movie, play, or ballet.

THE PURSUIT OF HAPPINESS— A JOURNEY, NOT A DESTINATION

In a discussion about retirement, one of the participants, Sally, told me her story. Sally retired for the first time at age 12! When she was a child figure skating star, her mother had a fight with the instructor and pulled Sally out of the program and the competition. According to Sally, she had been on the way to stardom. This involuntary retirement was painful at first, but eventually she was relieved, because she realized that serious figure skating required more of a commitment than she was willing to make. She went on to become a teacher and, many years later, retired from her job.

Now Sally is a happy retiree, thanks to being vitally involved in writing a novel that's currently in the hands of a literary agent. Sally has always liked to write, but this is her first attempt at fiction. The process of creating and telling a story has made her happy. She'll be delighted if the book is published, but her focus has been instead on "getting the novel right." She told me, "I was a star at 12 and don't need that any more."

Willa Bernhard, a retired therapist and colleague, was looking for a project after she retired. She became fascinated with women's experiences with aging, retirement, and life after 60. She easily found women who were eager to discuss their experiences and the unexpected joys and challenges that came with retirement. Bernhard presented her findings before a group of 20 friends. The enthusiastic response led her to consider writing a book about the freedom these women felt as they began expressing facets of themselves that had been dormant.

Bernhard is not certain that she will write a book. At first, she felt guilty, thinking she'd failed because she had not produced one. But she realized that focusing on the end product was detracting from the happiness she derived from interacting with the women, and that just the process of meeting fascinating women who keep expanding their horizons has given her happiness. She is continuing to do the interviews and remains engaged, and she may or may not return to the idea of a book.

These stories underscore the point made by a leading scholar of happiness, Professor Ed Diener. In a personal communication with me, he wrote, "What leads to long-term happiness is pursuing that next goal. . . . The pursuit of happiness might actually be true long-term happiness."[18]

Living an Engaged Life With a Purpose

There are those like Albert Schweitzer who believe that "the only ones among you who will be really happy are those who have sought and found how to serve."[19] Psychiatrist Gene Cohen confirmed this view of happiness in his 5-year study of 100 adults over 60, which included more than 1,000 hours of interviews. He found over and over again that people want to be more active, more engaged, and more stimulated. This is the result of an inner push.[20] This engagement can take the form of working part time, participating in an educational program, or volunteering. The individuals he studied wanted, for the most part, to be engaged but with more opportunity to control their own schedule and have a certain amount of autonomy. Cohen further found evidence that engagement in long-term activities, like a book club that meets on a regular basis, can be more satisfying than lots of "one-shot activities."

Leading a Contemplative Life

The Dalai Lama, who has been called by many "the high priest of happiness," suggested that we concentrate on our inner world as a way to "make ourselves happier and also transform society."[21] He suggested that lasting happiness does not depend on material things, job titles, and other external tags: "The acquisition of material goods, financial security, power, and fame may lead to happiness, but it too is transient . . . when those stimuli cease, the associated pleasure wanes."[22] Lasting happiness depends on knowing yourself and paying attention to your life as you attempt to find inner peace and balance.

Cathy, a successful businesswoman, seemed to have it all. She and her husband had done well in commercial real estate. They were now at the point in their lives when they could retire and start giving back to the community. She joined various boards and raised money for the arts community. Cathy commented,

> I enjoyed being retired and being active in the community. What I didn't have was inner peace. I tried traditional religion but found that most of what I have been told to take on faith was inconsistent, irrational, and unfulfilling. I have been on a 25-year quest to find what it was that I felt was missing.

Through friends, she discovered a class about Kabbalah, a spiritual philosophy based in Judaism, that deals with universal questions from ancient times. Those who study Kabbalah struggle to understand the purpose of the universe and how each person fits in. Cathy ended our conversation by pointing out

> you can have all the money in the world but have an empty life. Now that I have found Kabbalah, I take the time to be in the present, to meditate, to focus on my spiritual life. No matter what happens, I think I will be able to take it in my stride. Am I happy? Yes, very much so.

Cathy still serves on boards, but she now makes time for her spiritual quest.

Emotional Happiness—Feeling Happy

Maybe the simplest way to think about happiness is to ask yourself how you feel. Does a certain activity or thought make you feel happy? Gilbert wrote, "Happiness, then, is the you-know-what-I-mean feeling" often tied to an experience today or a desire about the future. He claimed that "there is no simple formula for finding happiness," nor do we have the "ability to project ourselves forward in time."[23] Thus the conundrum: We intuitively feel entitled to happiness, and we know what it is when we feel it, but we cannot predict what will make us happy. This observation led to the title of his book, *Stumbling on Happiness*.

CONCLUSION: MATTERING AND HAPPINESS

So where does that leave us in understanding the relationship of mattering and happiness? What do mattering and happiness have in common? Theorists see both concepts as motives explaining human behavior. We are driven by the need to feel happy and to be appreciated. Rosenberg studied the need to matter as a motivator for behavior. He described a boy who had threatened suicide, but because he felt he mattered to his theater club at school, he skipped school but sneaked into school play rehearsals.[24] Similarly, Gilbert pointed out that Freud, following in the footsteps of Plato, Aristotle, Hobbes, and Mill, suggested that humans strive toward happiness and that this striving influences their behavior.[25] People are motivated when they feel they matter (e.g., adult learners remain in school when the policies and practices of the institution are responsive to them) and will keep at a task or thought if they believe it will make them happy.

Paula, a former editorial writer for a major newspaper, found that retirement for her combined the intertwining of happiness and mattering. Her newspaper offered some top reporters the opportunity to take advantage of a buyout. Part of the buyout included an 18-month stipend for any employee who located a setting in which to contribute to society. Always interested in hospital work, Paula found a volunteer job in the emergency room of a local hospital. After the stipend ended, she explained why she continued her work: "At the paper, I was always in the midst of arguments with staff. Now patients see me and say, 'You are an angel.' " When she wrote me about her experience, she described herself as "happy": "I am lucky to have a good marriage. I love having four grandchildren with whom I am very involved, and I feel appreciated and depended upon at the hospital. What more could you ask for?"

We may tell ourselves that we want to engage in a purposeful life, that we want to pursue happiness, or that we want to feel we still matter. However, this does not happen by chance.

IT'S YOUR TURN: YOUR MATTERING AND HAPPINESS SCORES

Most of us probably don't spend much time analyzing whether we matter to others or whether we're happy. We just live day to day. Now is the time to become intentional in thinking about mattering and happiness. Now that you've seen how these two aspects of life are related, review your results on the Mattering Worksheet (Exhibit 1.1, p. 36) and the Subjective Happiness Scale (Exhibit 1.2, p. 44) to get an idea of how you are doing. If your mattering and happiness scores are not what you want, you can change them. The rest of the book suggests ways for you to design your life so that you feel that you matter and so that you can achieve happiness.

2

Check Your Psychological Portfolio

Most of us would agree that we strive to be happy and that we need to feel we matter to others and that our lives count for something. How do we make all of this happen? There is no sure-fire method or guarantee, but as the title of this book suggests, there are strategies we can use to revitalize our resources.

We need to revitalize our Identity, reassess our Relationships, and recast our Purpose—all aspects of our psychological portfolio described in the introductory chapter of this book. A strong psychological portfolio provides the infrastructure for a happy retirement.

The late Zandy Leibowitz and I produced a five-part NBC television series called *Caught-in-Between: Issues of Adult Development*.[1] One of the segments, "Starting Over," focused on two retired football heroes and several women returning to school after their children had left home.

David, a quarterback for an NFL team, appeared in "Starting Over." He had injured his knee and was forced into early retirement. When he had to retire, David lost his Identity. He had been part of a close-knit team with a strong sense of all for one and one for all. He said, "My buddies were my team. Now that I am off the team, what will happen to the team, and to me?" In addition to his shaky Identity, David's Relationship with his wife was clearly tense. His wife, also on the show, complained that at the end of her work day, "I come home and have to pick up David's ego." David also wondered about his Purpose: "Will I ever feel like a person again? How will I earn this much money again, and what will I do that gives me the total thrill I get from the game?" If we assessed his portfolio when he was playing football, we would rate his Identity, Relationships, and Purpose as very strong. After his injury, however, his ratings dropped dramatically to very weak.

Brig, another retired football star on the show, provided an interesting contrast. He had spent years slowly preparing for the future. By the time he retired, he had a law degree and segued into work with a new Identity, new set of Relationships, and new Purpose. He became a legal consultant to a trade association and formed a real estate company that helped professional athletes relocate.

The homemakers on the show expressed concerns similar to those of the football players. Their Identities had been totally wrapped up in their roles as family managers, parents, and wives. When their children grew up and left home, the women, like the athletes, were forced to confront questions about who they were now. They, too, were faced with how to structure their time and lives, become part of new communities, and develop a new raison d'être.

One woman on the show, Linda, told us she had loved being the "best parent in the school," the one to whom other mothers and children gravitated. Linda had been president of the parent–teacher association, a post just as time consuming and engaging as a full-time, salaried job. Her life was tied up with the school—her friends were other parents, and her social life revolved around families in the school community. Linda knew she needed help planning for the future, but she was so involved with committee meetings, school functions, and carpooling that she had no time or energy for planning. When she finally had time to contemplate the future, she saw each part of her Psychological Portfolio diminishing.

Her experience of retirement from full-time mother was similar to that of the football players. The drop in her portfolio was not as dramatic as David's, because she was still involved in parenting—readying her children for college. But she realized that she was at a crossroads and soon would have to craft a life separate from her children. At that point, she would have to revisit the issue of her Purpose in life.

Even though many of us cannot identify with professional athletes, or perhaps even with homemakers, their experiences provide a vivid example of how the psychological portfolio works. In the case of the athletes, because of the physical limitations that come with age, most are forced to transition from their true love to a Plan B. In addition to recognizing the advantages of their generous incomes, they have a deep identification with themselves as athletes. Their question: Will they be resilient when they can no longer say, "I am a quarterback"?

"Starting Over" portrayed the following concerns, echoed by many I interviewed:

- "Who am I? I feel that I am no longer of any use."
- "I have to work on marital relationships because we are now eyeball to eyeball."
- "I have lost my buddies. I have to adjust to not seeing as many people each day."
- "I am struggling to regain my sense of purpose."

A survey of Barnard College graduates who were transitioning to retirement confirmed the psychological challenges that accompany retirement. The study documented these women's need to discuss their identities and ways to restructure their lives.[2] They expressed the need to gain a new identity and master new challenges.

If people thought as much before retiring about ways to revitalize their Identity, Relationships, and Purpose after retirement as they do about their financial well-being, they might have a better handle on this major transition. Over and over, I have heard or read the same refrain: "We thought it was all about money, but now we see it is much more. Retirement is a *big* transition that includes major changes." To handle this big transition, it is important to understand each part of your Psychological Portfolio.

VIEW YOUR IDENTITY

When asked to name the biggest challenge facing them in retirement, many reported that losing their Identity was number one. Giving up your title and mission can shake your sense of self. How do you identify yourself when you meet someone? For many, it's threatening to try to answer the question, "Who am I without my job?" even though we know Identity is much more than your job.

Your *Identity*—who you are—is an overall term referring to what you do, your personality characteristics, and even how you see the world. When we say, "I am a lawyer," "I am a contractor," "I am a teacher," or "I am a homemaker," we're defining ourselves by what we do. When we say, "I am a caring person" or "I am assertive," we're defining ourselves by our personality or character. Because so many people use their work role as their identifying tag to the world, what happens when that tag no longer applies?

You might be an adult child, a parent, a sibling, or a friend, or you might be identified with a spiritual, religious, or educational endeavor, yet you have a sense of self that cuts across all of your roles. According to Daniel Levinson, author of *The Seasons of a Man's Life*, your identity is the sum of the roles you play and the behavioral characteristics you display. Your identity is your life structure, which combines the inner sense of self with the outer life you live.[3] He studied men, but the construct of identity applies to both men and women—though it may be played out in different ways.

Ruthellen Josselson, professor of psychology and author, studied college women's identity and explained *identity* as "our sameness-as-ourselves in containing our life story . . . [which] evolves and changes over time as we grow."[4] It is the core of self, "the backbone of a life story [that] provides unity to a life as lived."[5] She continued, "Identity is what we make of ourselves. In forming and sustaining our identity, we build a bridge between who we feel ourselves to be internally and who we are recognized as being by our social world."[6]

Josselson's first book, *Finding Herself: Pathways to Identity Development in Women*, reported how 60 college seniors from four colleges and universities emerged from their childhood to young adulthood. Some were tied forever to their parents' standards; others reworked childhood identities to achieve a new, independent sense of self; some were stuck because of too many choices; and others were in a constant state of confusion. Josselson used the word *anchoring* to describe metaphorically what happened as the college women she studied separated from their childhood and were revising their identities.[7] She followed up with these women 12 years later to see how they had revised their lives. Despite the different paths they had taken, they were all concerned with new ways to express their connections with others and their growing sense of competence.

Like these women, some retirees—whether a 35-year-old football player or a 65-year-old CEO—are stuck in their former work and family identities, others are confused by too many choices, and still others are able to move ahead and achieve a new place of comfort. Josselson's study of how college women's identity developed over time is instructive because the students, like retirees, were leaving the familiar and moving into the unknown. Many retirees fear that their competence might diminish and wonder about the inevitable changes in their relationships with others.

Retirement is one of those times that require a new sense of self and a new way of living in the world. A former college dean who participated in one of my retirement focus groups said, "I no longer know who I am, so I find I am building a fence around myself for protection." When others in the group asked him to explain, he responded, "I never ask any more what someone did before retirement because I do not want to be reminded of who I was." Another man, a former plumber, had enjoyed constant calls from his clients telling him how desperate they were and how much they needed him to save the day. "I admit I miss being needed," he confessed.

These men were struggling to find new anchors, new ways of continuing their life stories, and new ways of seeing themselves as they left their full-time work. Those who can modify their former identity and incorporate a new sense of self and new life structure demonstrate resilience—the ability to bounce back from negative experiences. Resilient individuals "turn disruptive changes and conflicts from potential disasters into growth opportunities. This is the heart of resilience. It's like finding the silver lining in the cloud."[8]

VIEW YOUR RELATIONSHIPS

Relationships play a critical role in your psychological portfolio. According to an AARP study, most people over 60 do not move to a different state for a simple reason—they want to stay near their family and friends.[9] Researchers have found that between 1985 and 2004, the size of people's intimate circles and number of "close confidantes" decreased significantly and that there has been a shift away from ties in the neighborhood; voluntary associations; community; and kin, especially spouses.[10] In 1985, respondents said they had approximately three confidantes with whom they could discuss personal or important matters. By 2004, they reported having barely two confidantes on average, and almost half of those studied discussed intimate and important issues with only one other person or kept everything inside. Researchers have found that lessening ties with community and voluntary groups weakens one's sense of well-being. In fact, that was the essence of Putnam's findings reported in *Bowling Alone: The Collapse and Revival of American Community*.[11]

Many retirees are very busy—volunteering, joining groups that engage in a wide variety of activities, and going out to dinner or the theater with friends. It's not unusual to hear a retiree say, "I don't know how I had the time to work." But filling up your time with activities is not the same as being happy.

According to author and psychiatrist Gene Cohen, many retirees have busy social lives but still feel unfulfilled. He continually asked those he studied, "What gives you a sense of meaning in your life?" He found that retirees need a variety of relationships—short term and long term, meaningful as well as transient—to provide balance in life. Meaningful activities could include participating in a walking group that meets regularly; transient activities are more ad hoc, such as going to a single lecture. Cohen described a *social portfolio*, suggesting that it is similar to a financial portfolio. His advice was first, to diversify by engaging in a combination of group activities and individual pursuits; second, to make sure the combination of activities will provide the supports necessary to protect oneself against future losses; and third, to start building this social portfolio long before retirement.[12]

One way to clarify the impact of retirement on the quality and quantity of your relationships is through the lens of time. According to sociologist Phyllis Moen, time structures our lives. In her book *It's About Time: Couples and Careers*, she viewed time from a life course perspective. We can go from being overwhelmed during the years when time is at a premium—as we were balancing work and family—to being underwhelmed in retirement if we do not have enough to do. For some, there is not enough time to do everything they want to do; for others, there is too much time to do the little they have planned.[13]

Moen articulated what we all know—that our lives our linked with others. When one person retires, the entire family is affected. A helpful way to think about these changes is to list the people with whom you had relationships before retirement and then make another list after retirement. One woman listed the following, in order of time spent with each: teen-age children, husband, work colleagues, church friends, and exercise acquaintances. Several years into retirement, her list had changed: her disabled father, church friends, husband, adult children, and doctors. In other words, as your life changes, the types of people you interact with change as well, as do the amount and quality of time you spend with them.

At Work

We try to figure out what will replace our paycheck, but we usually don't think about ways to replace what sociologists and economists refer to as our *social capital*—the network of relationships we derive from our work routine.[14] People may say, "I could afford to go on that trip, but I don't want to dip into capital." Their financial capital provides security for the future and generates income for living. Social capital is analogous: Your ties at work, your community of colleagues, your intellectual community, your personal relationships—all

62

protect you against loneliness and bolster your sense of well-being.

For most people, work provides a physical place to go most days and regular contacts with others. Even people who work at home usually have a routine that brings them into contact with others, whether through conference calls, an occasional meeting, or lunch with friends in the neighborhood. But something happens to this routine when you retire.

Ben is an example of someone who discovered that his former colleagues were no longer interested in him. An outgoing person whose lifetime career had been in human resources, he expected his professional relationships to continue when he retired. He was startled and sad as he reported on some unexpected changes:

> My work relationships changed almost immediately. I was not needed anymore. I received an occasional call to ask about what I had done about this and that, where had I filed something, and then, after a few months, the phone didn't ring and the e-mails stopped. I was invited to attend a former colleague's retirement party. I went, but was uncomfortable with the tone of the chitchat. I had the feeling it was guardedly polite—I was clearly out of the loop. I really believed that my old work friends were friends and that those friendships would endure. The reality is that most of them are now cordial but distant. I have been slow to form another network—maybe I don't trust friendships unless they go back a long time.[15]

Ben is not an isolated case. Sociologist Robert Weiss found that the 69 men and women in his sample felt isolated after experiencing the losses of challenging work and participation in a work community. He wrote,

> It can be experienced as a world gone quiet, as having been exiled from the active social world, as not being wanted. . . . Without membership in a social network, there are no invitations to outings. . . . The discomfort of social isolation disappears when the people who were isolated become engaged in social activity.[16]

With Friends and Family

Inevitably, you will spend less time—or maybe no time at all—with work buddies. That leaves more time to spend with friends, family, and partners. But this change is not always smooth. In a group discussion among policemen about retirement, they reported having no concerns until I commented, "I am glad you are looking forward to retirement, which includes spending 24/7 with your partners or spouses." Several groaned and then began to reveal some of their fears about the future, especially related to how they would spend their hours and what it would be like to spend much more time with their wives.

In Ben's case, his disappointment with work colleagues was mirrored by changes in his relationship with his wife:

> The relationship changes in my life have been a shocker! However, the biggest change at home has been with my wife. We used to love our weekends together—bike riding, day trips. Now if I am around the house too much during the week, she disappears on the weekend. As they say, "for better or worse, but not for lunch."

The day Larry retired from his job as plant manager, he saw the movie *About Schmidt*.[17] Jack Nicholson plays the part of a midlevel manager who has just retired. In the movie, the new retiree drops in at his old office to see if he can be of help. He gets the cold shoulder. Larry was particularly struck by Schmidt's wondering out loud who his wife really was and whether they even loved each other. The movie scared Larry. He felt a tremendous need to connect with his wife. In fact, he startled her when he said, "Now you're my best friend." What seemed like a joke is no joke. Ben and Larry and their wives faced one type of family issue: Potentially, the couples were going to be spending more time together. For many, this will force them to reexamine their relationship.

I asked the men in the Same Boat Group to describe the worst thing about retirement. The following comment highlights some of the stresses couples face:

> I found that the power base shifted in our marriage. There had been a subtle understanding that since I made more money, I had more power. Now that was changing. I wasn't listened to as I used to be. . . . Our power conflict is over territoriality. I used to have my own office. Now we share an office and a computer. We are constantly interrupting each other, vying for the computer. I am sure the solution is simple, but we cannot agree on how to solve it. I think the arguments about space are a metaphor for our relationship.

Although it may not seem obvious ahead of time, retirement can also raise issues about your relationship with other family members than your life partner. Now that you have more time, how do you balance your own life with the needs of your children and grandchildren? Should you move to another area to be close to your family? How do you manage to do this without disrupting their lives? And how do you balance your social life and the needs, and sometimes demands, of adult children? There is a great deal of fantasizing about how family will fill the void during retirement. To the surprise of one couple I interviewed, after they moved to be near family, their adult children moved because of a great career opportunity. The parents felt stuck in a community they did not know.

One couple expressed guilt because they were living a life of freedom. Their daughter was upset that they did not babysit regularly. During one intergenerational focus group, a retired woman said, "I don't expect my adult children to disrupt their lives for me—as long as they come to dinner every Friday night." The rest of the group laughed, and her daughter-in-law sighed.

Other Relationship Issues

In general, women live longer than men and are more likely to live alone in their later years. The issue of loneliness was a common one for members of the Retirement Seminar Group, an informal group of women who formed to support each other as they negotiated their retirement transition. "It is hard to have no one to react to your thoughts, or to care if you return on time. You need someone to talk trivia with," one member said. "There is good news and bad news," added another participant: "You have to make your own decisions." Another woman chimed in, "I'm fine during the day, but it's at night that loneliness sets in. I am uncomfortable eating alone at night."

Social life and friendships often revolve around more than the personal contacts and schedule at the office, plant, or store. When you stop working and change your routine, there's a good chance you'll also experience a shift in your relationships with friends and the broader community. You may replace your 7 a.m. visits to the health club with a workout at 10 a.m. or 2 p.m. Suddenly, you realize that none of the pals you used to swim or lift weights with are around at that time. Or instead of going to the office cafeteria for coffee, you may start to hang out at the corner coffee shop, only to realize it's filled with 20-somethings who are working on their laptops. The challenge you'll face is how to develop new, meaningful relationships within the parameters of your new routine and activities.

VIEW YOUR PURPOSE

Creating a happy retirement depends on finding or choosing a life that gives you a new reason to get up in the morning. The challenge is to uncover your passion and choose activities and priorities that make you feel you matter.

Marc Freedman, founder and president of Civic Ventures and founder of the Experience Corps, the largest national service program for Americans age 50 and older, is a leading proponent of what he has called *civic engagement*. The idea came to him after he realized that although retirees between 55 and 70 were delighted with their freedom, often they felt "a powerful sense of loneliness . . . [and lack of] a sense of purpose" in addition to loss of the bonds they'd forged with coworkers.[18]

He started Civic Ventures to help people find "new life in so-called retirement, underscoring the power of purpose and illustrating the wide range of possibilities for significant engagement in later life" by offering them opportunities to serve their community and therefore "strengthen civil society."[19] His most recent book, *Encore: Finding Work That Matters in the Second Half of Life*, promotes the goal of reinventing your career to make a better world and feel better about yourself.[20]

More recently, Civic Ventures, with grants from the Atlantic Philanthropies and the John Templeton Foundation, started awarding an annual Purpose Prize of $100,000 to five "social entrepreneurs over 60 years of age who are role models for engaged retirement." One 2007 award went to Conchy Bretos in Miami, an advocate for improved public housing. She helped develop a model program that addressed the needs of residents in public housing. Marilyn Gaston, a physician, and Gayle Porter, a clinical psychologist, were honored for improving the health of midlife African American women. They founded Prime Time Sister Circles, which provides facilitators, a curriculum, and other tools to help women improve their health and overcome some of the diseases most common in their communities. These and other inspirational volunteers are described on the Civic Ventures Web site (http://www.civicventures.org).

We all know retirees or preretirees who say that they love *not* having a purpose—living day to day, choosing their friends and routines for the pure enjoyment they offer. One man told me,

> I am happy doing nothing. I am into sloth. Everybody asks what I am doing. I feel like saying, "as little as possible." I am reminded that after the women's movement, housewives felt guilty if they were not out there conquering the world. That is the way I feel. My success is evaluated [by others] by the degree to which I keep busy doing worthwhile activities.

The decision to "do nothing" is perfectly appropriate for some people, especially if they feel they've been denied the time and opportunity for recreation and relaxation during their working and family-raising years. However, most of those I interviewed felt that it was critical to have a defined purpose in retirement.

I interviewed Jack, a devoted public servant and former U.S. cabinet official who had a highly visible career. True, he enjoyed being in the limelight, but his work was always in the public interest. After retiring from government 20 years ago, he went into private consulting work to help companies that were faltering. He was the consummate problem solver.

After retiring from public service, Jack raised funds to start a public interest center as part of a university.

This provided him with a place to go, a continuing identity, and a feeling of usefulness. In addition to center activities, he was writing his autobiography and was constantly thinking about what stories to include, what narrative to emphasize. He could talk for hours about his experiences with different companies, showing how he was able to bring all the parties together to resolve the issues.

Jack shared his concerns about his forthcoming retirement from consulting work. As he talked, I heard humor, dedication, and an overriding theme of being a savior. He lit up when discussing the book. Unfortunately for him, the book project would be completed in less than a year. I could hear some uncertainty in his voice when he talked about his future. At that point, I drew three columns of equal height labeled "Identity," "Relationships," and "Purpose." I asked him to point to the column that would be most problematic for him after his book project was completed. He tapped vigorously on the column labeled "Purpose" and said,

> The center is no longer viable at the university, so I will no longer have that as a base. In addition, I do not have the energy I once had. I will really retire for the first time. By this time next year, the center will be closed and my book completed. I have no idea what to do. I can only tolerate golf once in a while. Actually, you have hit on what has been eating me up this past year. I can lecture, now and then, at the university, but I need more than that. I need something that will engage my energy and make me feel useful and happy. That is my challenge.

Allen, a 60-year-old photographer, retired and moved to a new city because of a wonderful job opportunity for his wife. His wife's work gave him the opportunity to retire—something he had been considering for health reasons. Relieved to let go of running an office, Allen assumed that he could find part-time work. When no one would hire him, he attributed the rejections to age bias. He constantly thought about where he could find any opportunity that would allow him to engage in creative work. He was depressed and very much at sea trying to figure out what to do next. Eventually, he became active in his condominium association and took pictures of apartments for realtors. He also took pictures for several friends who were publishing books. However, he felt he was not busy enough and wondered if he would ever recapture his zest for living.

Jack, the public servant, and Allen, the photographer, both confronted the reality that retirement was changing their lives. Their challenge is to figure out how to enjoy and contribute in the coming years. Like them, your purpose may be tied to your job and/or family. When your purpose is interrupted, it's time to embark on a period of searching for a new way to live your life that will make you happy. In Part II of this volume, "How Others Have Found Happiness," I discuss tools and strategies that others have used to meet this major challenge. But before availing yourself of these strategies, an examination of your psychological portfolio can help you identify any areas in need of attention.

VISUALIZE YOUR PSYCHOLOGICAL PORTFOLIO

You can visualize your Psychological Portfolio as being composed of three columns, each representing a portion of your resources—Identity, Relationships, and Purpose. As you think about retirement, rate each part of your portfolio as 1 for *very weak,* 2 for *in the middle,* or 3 for *very strong* in Exhibit 2.1.

If you feel that your Identity is strong, check the box in the first row; if you feel it is OK, check the box in the middle row; and if you feel it is very low, check the box in the bottom row. If you are already retired, rate where you are today and compare it with where you were. If you are not yet retired, rate where you are today and think about what you will need as you plan ahead.

EXHIBIT 2.1. Your Psychological Portfolio

Think about retirement, and place a check mark in the appropriate box for each part of your portfolio.

Rating	Identity: I know myself.	Relationships: I have enough friends and supports.	Purpose: I know where I am going.
3 (*very strong*)			
2 (*in the middle*)			
1 (*very weak*)			

To see how this rating system works, let's look at the example of Martha. She had been managing a top restaurant for 25 years, but the place was becoming an octopus, enveloping her. Burned out and needing to do something different, she retired precipitously without giving much thought to her next steps. Martha's husband, Lance, was a construction worker who felt he could work anywhere. They began to dream of running their own bed and breakfast. Martha could cook, and Lance could rebuild or renovate any house they bought. They sold their house and moved to Washington State. After renting for several months, they found and bought just the right house to turn into the bed and breakfast. It sounded ideal—they had a dream, they were on the same page, and they were making it happen.

For the first couple of months, getting the house fixed up and organizing the bed and breakfast was fun. But then Martha began to ask herself, "What have I done? Why have I done this?" She was happy about leaving the stress of her restaurant job but found it difficult to cope with so many life changes. They had left their jobs, shifted their identities from employees to entrepreneurs, and suddenly found themselves together 24 hours a day, 7 days a week. They had moved out of state, losing friends and close family connections as well as relationships with coworkers. Their daily routines were completely in flux, and on top of that, they faced the stress of creating a new business, with all the financial anxiety that accompanies such an endeavor. Martha and Lance knew that one shouldn't try to take on too

EXHIBIT 2.2. Martha's Psychological Portfolio Before Retiring

Rating	Identity	Relationships	Purpose
3 (very strong)	✓	✓	
2 (in the middle)			
1 (very weak)			✓

many transitions simultaneously. However, they were so eager to make it happen that they did exactly that.

Martha filled out a chart before retiring (Exhibit 2.2) and 1 year after retiring (Exhibit 2.3). Before retiring, she explained, "I had clarity about my identity and purpose and a strong sense of community, plus a network of friends as well as adult children. The only negative was my feeling of being burned out." She rated both Identity and Relationships as *very strong* (3), reflecting her solid relationships at work and in the community. Her Purpose, however, she rated *very weak* (1), reflecting her desire to leave what she was doing and make a change.

EXHIBIT 2.3. Martha's Psychological Portfolio After Retiring

Rating	Identity	Relationships	Purpose
3 (very strong)			✓
2 (in the middle)		✓	
1 (very weak)	✓		

A year after retirement, Martha's portfolio had changed radically. Although she had a new purpose—to create a successful bed and breakfast—she was unclear about her Identity, and her Relationships were in flux. The strength of these two parts of her portfolio was greatly reduced (see Exhibit 2.3).

Martha felt she had made a decision that could be difficult and costly to reverse, and she was scared. She and Lance had been fortunate to have a joint goal and a new adventure together. But they felt they had taken too many risks. It would have been wiser to test the waters in the new community before moving, to make sure they could make the dream come true. They had needed a business plan, as well as plans about ways to meet people. If you do what they did—retire, move, and start a major new activity such as a business, all at the same time—you could be asking for trouble.

I really empathized with Martha and Lance, because my experiences were similar. My husband and I both retired and moved hundreds of miles from where we had lived for more than 30 years. Soon I realized I'd initiated too many transitions at once. Things were not going well; in fact, I was flunking retirement. An analysis of my portfolio showed that I no longer had a tag to explain my Identity to others and myself, was not clear about how to develop a meaningful network of Relationships, and lacked a Purpose. I was amazed. It never occurred to me that I, a transition expert, would have such difficulty! All three parts of my portfolio needed to be strengthened.

I focused on Purpose, thinking that if I found one, I would regain my Identity. My solution was to follow the path of my previous career. I had always written books about transitions, so it made sense to write a book about the transition I myself was experiencing in retirement. The process of writing the book, finding a publisher, and fine-tuning the manuscript took several years and gave me a focus, a sense of self, and a reason to function.

Rebuilding Relationships was a complex challenge. On one hand, I had the support of my husband of 40 years. We were in this together. But I had moved away from close friends and other family members. So though I was in a meaningful relationship with my husband, there were big gaps. It took me several years to feel I belonged to my new community. I tried serving on the boards of several local organizations, but this was unsatisfying because most boards expect you to raise money, and fundraising is not my strength. That endless process of searching for the right activity seemed doomed to failure, and after 5 years, I retreated from board activities, realizing that I preferred working on a project rather than serving as a board member.

When an acquaintance called and invited me to join yet another advisory group, my first answer was "no." But the power of invitation prevailed. She convinced me that the focus of the group was right up my alley because the mission of the organization, SCOPE, was to make Sarasota, Florida—with its large retiree population—a place where people of all ages matter. I helped SCOPE organize three major conferences on aging. We brought in creative experts who helped us figure out ways to make Sarasota a community for all generations. Working with SCOPE has been a rewarding experience and has made me feel I matter.

As I write this book, my Purpose and Identity are strong. However, I still miss what sociologist Robert Weiss missed—a place to go, an office where I belong, a place that becomes part of the structure of my week. I am also aware that as I get older, my professional shelf life is limited, and in the future I will have to revisit my entire portfolio and create a new path. And perhaps that is exactly the point: One's life goes on, one's portfolio changes, and one continues to adjust.

CONCLUSION: BACK TO MATTERING AND HAPPINESS

I have made the case that in retirement, there is a chance that you will no longer feel that you matter. I also assume that if you have your Identity, Relationships, and Purpose in order, you will have a better chance at happiness. This chapter has addressed several questions: How will you deal with your Identity, once your identifying tag is gone? Do you know how you will build new Relationships while nurturing the old? How will you design a life for yourself that gives meaning and a sense of Purpose?

This chapter has described your Psychological Portfolio. Looking ahead to Part II of this book, you will see the many ways people have strengthened all three facets of their portfolios.

It's Your Turn: Questions to Ask Yourself

Are you ready to consider your own Psychological Portfolio? You might never have labeled your resources in that way, but now is the time to start examining them by thinking about your Identity, Relationships, and Purpose—whether you are considering retirement or are already into it.

I am not promoting a particular lifestyle in retirement. In fact, I believe that there is no one path that is right for everyone. What I am promoting is that to be able to follow the path you want, it is important to have a strong psychological portfolio.

Here are some questions that may help you find some answers. Answer yes or no to each of the following:

Your Identity

- Do you have a sense of self, and do you matter to yourself?
- Do you feel you matter to others?
- Are you comfortable saying, "I'm retired" or "I'm considering retirement"?

Your Relationships

- Do you belong to a community that can substitute for your work community?

- Do you have someone with whom to share your daily life and innermost thoughts?
- Has retirement changed your personal relationships in unexpected ways?

Your Purpose

- Do you have a sense of purpose, a reason to get up in the morning?
- Do you have a place to go where you're expected and valued?
- Do you have any ideas about how to develop a new sense of purpose?

If your answers were all "yes," your portfolio is strong, and this bodes well for your future. If you answered "no" to some of the questions, start focusing on those areas. List below what you need to work on, and read the rest of the book with the goal of finding a roadmap to follow.

My Areas to Work On

1.
2.
3.

II

HOW OTHERS HAVE
FOUND HAPPINESS

3

Revitalize Your Identity

It is now time to focus on how others have revitalized their portfolios. This chapter raises the perplexing question, can adults change? And more specifically, can individuals change their Identity? I don't mean to walk on both sides of the question, but the answer is— it all depends.

George E. Vaillant, psychiatrist and director of the Harvard Study of Adult Development, followed several groups over time to determine if their defense mechanisms—their involuntary coping mechanisms—changed over time. His research team followed the lives of a group of Harvard students through middle and old age, rating them in terms of their use of mature coping mechanisms. Most of those labeled "well adjusted" as students remained well adjusted. However, a small group moved to "poorly adjusted" in old age. And those designated poorly adjusted in college remained, for the most part, poorly adjusted in old age. In his book *Aging Well*, Vaillant found that luck, aging, and nurturing relationships can lead to more mature ways to cope with life.[1] His work indicates that coping is relatively stable over time but that there are opportunities to change one's adaptive style, given the right combination of luck, good work and family environments, and therapy.

According to Paul Costa and Robert McCrae, directors of the Baltimore Longitudinal Study of Aging, the personality traits that differentiate one person from another—neuroticism, extroversion, openness to new experience, agreeableness, and conscientiousness— remain relatively constant over the course of one's life.[2] Once an extrovert, always an extrovert, whether working or retired; once eager to experience the unknown, always an adventurer; and so on. It might appear that a person has changed, but a changed appearance might reflect only external changes—one's work life, where one lives, and what one does with one's time.

Vaillant explained the seeming paradox that both "change and continuity are true" as follows:

> Our temperament . . . which comprises such personality elements as extroversion or introversion . . . does not change very much. . . . Character, however, does change. If one defines personality by an individual's adaptive style . . . then over time . . . [people can] outgrow and recover from restrictive environments.[3]

In other words, in most cases you can predict the future from the past, but there are instances when people change. As one therapist said, "If I did not believe that, why would I stay in practice?" That strikes me as good news.

Many of those I interviewed said that the greatest issue in retirement resided in the assault on their Identity. They were not discussing how they coped with life or whether they were resilient; they were discussing their jobs or external life. The research seems fairly clear: We can change our residences, our marriage partners, or our cities, but the way we cope with these changes is probably the way we have always coped with change.

Both our external and internal worlds are challenged when we retire. In this chapter, I share stories and examples of how retirees bolstered their inner and outer identities. They found various ways to discover and rediscover their identity as they adapted to changing circumstances. See if any of these speak to you.

CONSTRUCT A PERSONAL NARRATIVE

When you retire and no longer have a "real" job, it is harder to know how to describe yourself to the outside world. For some, it may be sufficient to say "retiree," but you'll probably be much happier if you strive to define a postretirement identity that can provide structure to your days and meaning to your life. If your identity in retirement is shaky or uncertain, think about how you want to present yourself to the outside world by thinking about what matters to you.

Toni, a clerical worker, created a story about herself that went from fiction to fact. She was introduced to a man who asked what she did. She lied and told him she was an interior designer. When he asked for her card, she felt trapped. How could she explain this lie? Then it came to her: Her lie was the window into her next path. She clearly did not like her current work identity and instead blurted out the work identity she actually wanted. Realizing this, she enrolled in a part-time course to become an interior designer, which she managed to complete while still working in an office.

What is the scenario you would like to see? Imagine writing a play about yourself in the future. Let your imagination soar; later, you can scale down to some realistic goals. Your challenge is to identify many ways to develop new anchors—new ways of being when old labels no longer work.

For those struggling with the future meaning of their lives in retirement, "constructing a meaningful narrative identity" and "weighing different hypothetical possibilities" are ways to figure out what's next.[4] Dan P. McAdams, professor of psychology and human development at Northwestern University, is among a growing number of psychologists using *narrative psychology*—listening to stories and storytelling—to better understand the lives of adults and help them construct more effective futures. He studied the plot line that ran through the stories of "ordinary" people, superstars, and historical figures, all of whom had experienced overwhelming challenges that they overcame through strategies such as therapy, reading, meditation, or studying. I think this explains our fascination with memoirs of individuals overcoming overwhelming challenges.

McAdams suggested that individuals can reflect on their lives to identify their story line and connect it to their future.[5] One of my interviewees, Maggie, a former investigative reporter for a major paper, did just that. Much younger than her husband, she took early retirement and together they moved to a new community. While she had worked, she had an outlet through her newspaper to write about whatever she uncovered. Some of her colleagues were dismayed that she had opted for early retirement. They kept asking her what she would do.

In truth, Maggie had trouble changing her self-definition from effective worker to person of leisure. When she described herself, it was always in the past tense through stories of how she had investigated scams and white-collar crime. She saw herself as someone who had thrived on solving puzzles. As Maggie projected her future, she imagined herself as someone who would get involved in her community and make a difference.

Unclear about the specifics, she began gaining confidence that she could turn her new life into something satisfying. It took a year or two before she found her spot. First, she became involved in her condominium association. Eventually, she was elected president and effectively led the fight to save adjoining land for a nature reserve. Following this, she and her husband became part of a small group that started a think tank designed to alert the community to issues of public concern. Maggie's projected scenario had helped her construct her future. Leaving her old identity as a journalist behind, she acquired a new one—political activist—and she found it just as satisfying.

SEARCH FOR A SPIRITUAL HOME

After retiring, Jill, who had been an elementary school teacher, volunteered to work on various projects, including one on oral history at the Holocaust Museum with Holocaust survivors, another for a library, and a third reading books to the blind. But none of these activities satisfied her. Her strong personality trait, openness to experience—in conjunction with serendipity—led her on a spiritual journey. She shared her quest with me:

> For many years, I had felt a spiritual hole, an emptiness in my center. While identified with a religion, I was nonpracticing. I felt aligned with my religion primarily by culture and values. I had no integrated core of spiritual knowledge, understanding, or beliefs.

One day, she attended a memorial service at a church. She described how she felt "blown away" by a young minister who impressed her as "exceptional, perceptive, and sensitive." She returned to the church. Over time, she got to know the ministers and started attending some religious education courses. Last year, Jill was invited to teach such a course. She described her over-all experience:

> By happenstance, I was introduced to a spiritual community honoring beliefs coinciding with my own. It provided a spiritual home in which I felt comfortable and warmly welcomed. . . . With possible difficult life tasks ahead and so much that is unknown, it is a comfort to have a foundation of spiritual beliefs and a group to share them with in facing whatever life will bring.

When I interviewed Jill about her spiritual journey, she said she believed that she finally encountered her path because she was open to it and ready for it. She agreed completely with the book *There Are No Accidents: Synchronicity and the Stories of Our Lives* by Robert Hopcke, whose premise is that what seems to be an accidental event—such as Jill's visiting the church for the first time—may not be a mere coincidence but rather a logical outgrowth of what has gone before.[6]

Similarly, Stanford professor John D. Krumboltz studied *planned happenstance*—the importance of being open to change as a result of chance occurrences. You never know what chance occurrence will trigger a new idea or life direction. The title of his book, *Luck Is No Accident: Making the Most of Happenstance in Your Life and Career*, says it all.[7] In Jill's view, her visit to the church for the memorial service was a chance occurrence that triggered a change in her life at a time when she was open to it. Several key themes of her life emerged in retirement: her openness to new challenges, her ability to look inward, her comfort in groups, her awareness of opportunities, and her desire to learn more about herself and her environment.

By happenstance, I met Ruth, an art historian, who represents another way to undertake a spiritual journey. When, by mutual agreement with her employer, she retired from her executive director position, she was frightened of losing her Identity. She *was* her job, and her job was her life. "I felt lost," she admitted. "I shopped, and shopped, and shopped. I was so unhappy that I did not want to look up former colleagues. Frankly, I was too embarrassed. I felt like a failure. I *was* a failure."

While browsing in a new age bookstore, she came across a tape about meditation. Intrigued, she bought the tape and tried using it to meditate at home. However, meditating on her own was unsatisfactory, so she attended a week-long meditation retreat where no talking was allowed. At first, the experience was unnerving. But by the end of the week, she looked in the mirror and saw that her face had fewer lines. Ruth joked, "The retreat was better than a Botox treatment."

This experience gave her the fortitude to accept what had happened in her job. "Without this, I would have felt as if I had fallen and was now depleted. Instead, the meditation helped me validate myself, to see the forced retirement transition as challenging, maybe even fun, but certainly not crushing." Ruth promised herself that she would never allow feelings of failure to overwhelm her again. In fact, she is endeavoring to share the experience of forging a new identity: She is studying to become a life coach.

The spiritual journey, for those who take the time to make it, pays off. Whether the strategy is joining a spiritual community, meditating, or doing yoga, the point is to clear your head of irrelevant matters, focus your energies, and be open to the peace that eventually will come. This transformation can occur at any time in life, but retirement presents a unique opportunity for reexamination of your life.

MODIFY YOUR AMBITION

After retirement, some people still yearn for their former role, power, or prestige. They have not given up the need to be center stage. That is understandable; when you have been at the top, you feel entitled to maintain your position as a leader and winner. One high-powered woman shared her feelings of rejection and irrelevancy with a friend, who wisely pointed out that her former successes were getting in her way. She could not let go of her expectations.

In his book *Ambition: How We Manage Success and Failure Throughout Our Lives*, Gilbert Brim, director of the MacArthur Foundation Research Network on Successful Mid-Life Development, proposed that retirees need to modify their ambition. Of course, that is easier said than done. Although it is important to keep dealing with challenges, you need to make them manageable. For those who have been highly successful, retiring can be particularly challenging. To succeed at retirement, you need to change your level of aspiration—maybe you don't need to be top dog. You also need to modify your goals—maybe you don't need to be the CEO but rather can take satisfaction from working on smaller projects as you reduce the time pressures on yourself.[8]

Gerry, for instance, has done just that. A former TV personality and member of the city council and several bank boards, she was a real player in her Midwestern town. Her identity was tied up in being heavily engaged in making a difference in her community. Suddenly, at age 50, she received the shock of her life—she was diagnosed with breast cancer. With good medical care, a positive attitude, a supportive family, and luck, she survived and was able to return to work. But after a year back in the thick of things, Gerry realized that her illness had been a wake-up call. She and her husband retired, moved to a warm climate, and chose to enjoy life at a slower pace.

Gerry, an extrovert, modified her ambition. She changed her timetables and goals. She no longer had the interest or energy to be a key player, to serve on paid boards, or to make videos for major companies. Still interested in contributing to the community, she wanted to do it on her own schedule and was satisfied with chairing a committee that addressed community issues and with serving as a social connector by entertaining friends and introducing them to each other.

I interviewed Tom, who had been a major player in the political arena and whose story is one of modified ambition. It was fascinating to learn about all the legislation he had initiated and his contributions to national policy. I asked Tom how he felt after he retired when he read about his past effectiveness. His answer: "I miss the shouting but feel I made a contribution. I am at peace with it." He came to see himself very differently and assumed his role as family historian seriously. He shifted his ambition from the public, political sphere to the personal, family sphere.

It is important to keep in mind that individuals vary in their ability to change and move away from center stage. Vaillant described this as the *maturing process*. However, those like Gerry who have characteristics like resilience and extroversion have a better chance at adapting to changing circumstances than others.

PRACTICE RESILIENCE

We all face circumstances, challenges, and opportunities requiring flexibility. Sam, a retired vice president of a trade association, is a perfect example of someone who hit a detour in his life plan but bounced back.

As a result of his interest in combining his business experience with coaching, and in preparation for retirement, he returned to school and obtained a PhD in counseling. His retirement plan was complete—to develop a Web site to serve baby boomers by providing information on issues concerning them such as health, new careers, and financial news. On the day he retired, Sam felt totally prepared, knowing that he was going to develop a business plan, secure a board of directors, and identify some sponsors to fund the project. Of the personality traits identified by Costa and McCrae,[9] Sam was low on neuroticism and high on extroversion, openness to new experience, agreeableness, and conscientiousness.

While Sam was developing the project, someone told him about a similar one that had just gone online. Someone had beaten him to the punch. He had a series of reactions. His first thought was, "This is terrible. I have spent the last few years on a fool's errand. Now what?" After some reflection, he felt relief that "now I don't have to raise the $10 million necessary to get the project off the ground." Then, considering the thought and effort he'd already put into the project, he asked himself, "Where is the white space in the project that beat me? What can I do that is not covered in the existing project?" At first, Sam was not sure what form his modified project would take, but he said, "Rest assured, it will happen." He did exactly what experts suggest: He demonstrated resilience by putting a major defeat into broader perspective, strategizing about ways to make it work for him, and developing a process for taking action.

There is a postscript to this story that shows again how resilient Sam has been. As I finished writing this book, I wrote to him to see how his project was coming along. He responded that after studying the research on boomers and the Internet and getting a better idea of the competition for his idea, he concluded that boomers

do not present a compelling picture for a sound business model and, therefore, would be of little interest to our potential investors. . . . So I'm now considering opportunities in both the nonprofit and for-profit sectors for my next wave. I realize that I am a living, breathing example of those boomers deciding what's next in their lives!"

I can't wait to see what identity he comes up with during his "next wave."

This raises the question of what we can do to become resilient in times of stress. There's no magic pill, but there are resources you can use. For example, psychologist Salvatore Maddi and his team studied the Illinois Bell Telephone company over a period of 10 years after the work force had been drastically reduced. Some of the managers crumbled under the stress, whereas others embraced change and moved on. Maddi and his team developed the Hardiness Institute, where people are trained to turn stressors into opportunities through "situational reconstruction" by imagining "alternative ways of thinking about the stressor."[10] Workbooks take the participant through a step-by-step process teaching ways to look at adversity, deal with it, and even grow from it.

The American Psychological Association's brochure *The Road to Resilience* points to resilience as a quality we can all adopt.[11] The brochure outlines 10 ways to build resilience:

1. "Make connections." Ask for help and give help.
2. "Avoid seeing crises as insurmountable problems." You might not be able to change your situation, but you can change the way you see it.

3. "Accept that change is a part of living." Focus on what you can change rather than what you cannot.
4. "Move toward your goals." Think in realistic terms. "What's one thing I know I can accomplish today that helps me move in the direction I want to go?"
5. "Take decisive actions. Act on adverse situations as much as you can."
6. "Look for opportunities for self-discovery."
7. "Nurture a positive view of yourself."
8. "Keep things in perspective."
9. "Maintain a hopeful outlook. . . . Try visualizing what you want, rather than worrying about what you fear."
10. "Take care of yourself." Be sure to relax, exercise, and have fun.

If you reread Sam's story, you will see he actually followed the APA guidelines for building resilience. You might consider using these 10 points as your resilience mantra.

TAKE INITIATIVE, TAKE CONTROL

When your life does not follow the script you wrote, you have a choice—to fold up your tent and retreat or to take the initiative and make something happen. Consider the many volunteers trying to find something meaningful to do. One retiree, formerly a high-powered lobbyist, called a coordinating volunteer organization and explained his interests and credentials. He finally received a call asking if he would like to ring the bell for the Salvation Army during the Christmas holidays—not exactly a role that fit with his concept of a new identity.

He realized that he'd have to take the initiative to figure out what he wanted to do—and do it. Actually, he joined Maggie, the former reporter, and helped start a local forum that sponsors programs at least twice a month to discuss major public issues. Open to the public, such meetings attract between 500 and 1,000 people.

It requires a great deal of gumption to keep searching until you find the place where you really feel useful. Persistence is essential as you take initiative.

I was personally the object of a retiree's initiative. Out of the blue, I received a letter from Robert, an associate dean of a graduate school at a major university, asking me to suggest productive and rewarding activities that he might explore when he moved to Sarasota. Noting that he was not interested in golf, he wanted recommendations about organizations he could join to meet local residents and about stimulating adult education courses. When Robert arrived in town, we had lunch together to discuss some opportunities that would help him become more involved in the community. Six months later, he was teaching music at a community college; had joined a church; was working as a volunteer with a theater group; and, he said, "having the time of my life." Again, his Identity as a person with initiative paid off.

TRY APPRECIATIVE INQUIRY

I met a woman named Laurie in a woman's support group that was focusing its discussion on Appreciative Inquiry (AI). Laurie told us that after her employer asked her to leave her administrative job, she retired and moved to another city with her husband. Fairly confident that her experience at a Fortune 100 company would open up part-time opportunities for her, she sent out a number of letters with her resume. The result was 100% rejections; either she was too qualified or not qualified enough. Understandably, Laurie was discouraged.

By chance, she heard of a workshop on AI that helped her mobilize her next steps. Codeveloped by David Cooperrider at Case Western Reserve University, AI is a method used to help organizations and individuals build on their strengths as they look to the future.[12] *Appreciative* refers to appreciating the strengths of the organization or person in question. *Inquiry* refers to searching, exploring, or investigating the positives in the person or organization. The underlying assumption is that individuals and organizations can continually grow if they ask the probing questions that will build on their strengths rather than their deficits. Very simply, the AI process begins with appreciating the present, then imagining an ideal future, and finally taking action.

After attending the workshop, Laurie reframed the experience of being rejected. She focused on her strengths and began to realize that she did not want a full-time job in an organization. As she said, "Been there, done that." She then imagined ways to create a new future. She gathered all her rejections and, on her computer, created a "rejection fan," a design that incorporated the texts of the many turndowns she had received. A former art major with a flair for color and design, she created a stunning computer image that reminded her of her talent and helped her realize that this was a strength she could build on.

She decided to embark on a new retirement career as a Web site designer. Eventually, Laurie replaced the "rejection fan" with an "opportunity fan." She now said to herself, "I matter to myself; I appreciate myself. Now let me dig deep and inquire about my earlier dreams, skills, and passions." She had applied AI to herself, and it seemed to be just what she needed to rediscover her Identity as a creative, artistic individual.

CONCLUSION

In our society, personal identity is tied more to our work than to any other facet of our life. By definition, the first thing to go when you retire is your work—and with it, often, your Identity. As we live longer and spend more years in retirement, the prospect of spending the rest of our lives confused about who we are and where we fit into the general scheme of things becomes a more severe problem, one that needs to be acknowledged and then responded to head on.

You might be saying to yourself, "That is all well and good, but I am not the kind of person who can take initiative and make things happen. I am too shy, too introverted, to do what Gerry or Sam did." This goes back to the question at the beginning of this chapter: Can you change? If you feel that your personality characteristics are holding you back, perhaps this is the time to seek help from a qualified counseling psychologist, career counselor, social worker, or other professional. No one ever said that change is easy, but we have just read, and will continue to read, about those who acknowledged the possible loss or diminishment of their identity in retirement and then moved ahead to do something about it.

IT'S YOUR TURN: TIPS ON HOW TO RESHAPE YOUR IDENTITY

Here are some exercises, based on the strategies used by people profiled in this chapter, to help you reshape your own identity in retirement.

1. Construct a Personal Narrative

Think about how you would describe yourself to others in the past and in the present. Now think about how you want to describe yourself in 10 years. Select an incident or theme that really captures the kind of person you have always been, and try to project how that story might play out in the future. If one of your life themes has been mending fences, consider how you might continue to be a force for peace. For example, you might become a mediator after obtaining the appropriate training.

2. Search for a Spiritual Home

If you're in turmoil as you leave a major role in your life, experiment with various options that may enable you to become more at peace with yourself, such as yoga, a religious group, or independent meditation or study.

3. Modify Your Ambition

Think about what you want to accomplish in your retirement years. For example, if you had been Teacher of the Year but put in 60 hours a week at school, you might not want to do that again. But it might be rewarding to spend 1 day a week as a tutor helping a child learn to read.

4. Practice Resilience

Think of a time or an incident in your life when you felt totally frustrated. Now, think of at least three things you could have done to circumvent the obstacles. Why not start a resilience support group? Brainstorming with others can give you fresh ideas.

5. Take Initiative, Take Control

Now that you're retiring, you may have to depend on yourself to reach out and create a life that matters for yourself and your family. Come up with three ways you can take initiative. If you can't think of any, imagine that you are coaching yourself. What would you suggest?

6. Try Appreciative Inquiry

Ask yourself some probing questions about your personal strengths and how you can use them to forge a new Identity in retirement. What about that art and design degree you never used because you found you could earn a better living as a stockbroker? Could you use your experience on Wall Street to write a textbook, or even a novel? What can you do if you have always been an automobile mechanic? Begin appreciating your strengths and seeing how they can be applied in numerous settings.

Tips You Will Follow

As you consider your own situation, list two or three tips you will follow in retirement so that you feel comfortable with your new identity. Read over the suggested tips and see if any fit you; if not, think of others that would fit. Remember, if you can feel comfortable with your identity, you are on the way to feeling that you matter.

Tip 1: _____

Tip 2: _____

Tip 3: _____

4

Revitalize Your Relationships

Retirement often interrupts the pattern of your personal and work relationships. The challenge is to figure out how to replace, maintain, and improve your social connections—your *social capital*—which in turn will result in feelings of well-being.[1] There are two major ways to think about building your social capital: First, substitute for what you lost on leaving work by making new connections, and second, revitalize your ongoing personal relationships. In that way, you will develop a social portfolio that will stand you in good stead.

MAKE NEW CONNECTIONS: INVEST IN SOCIAL CAPITAL

One of the best ways to make new connections, according to Malcolm Gladwell, author of *The Tipping Point: How Little Things Can Make a Big Difference*, is to identify *connectors*, or "people who link us up with the world . . . who introduce us to our social circles . . . on whom we rely more heavily than we realize . . . people with a special gift for bringing the world together."[2]

As young workers, we needed mentors to socialize us in the ways of our profession or occupation. As new retirees, we need connectors to join us with new people or activities to enrich our daily lives. Gladwell referred to the work of sociologist Mark Granovetter, who described two types of connectors: those with whom you have "strong ties," who are part of your social circle, and acquaintances with whom you have "weak ties" but who have access to a world you do not occupy. "Acquaintances, in short, represent a source of social power."[3] Both kinds of connectors will expand your social horizons.

Identify Your Connectors

Justin is an example of someone who took initiative and identified a connector who helped him change his retirement life. At one time, Justin managed a ski resort; later, he operated a marketing company. At the end of his career, he was the publisher of a chain of small monthly papers. When he turned 70, he sold the papers at 12 times what he paid for them. Justin's financial life was in order, and he was in a second marriage with a younger, working woman. They had twin boys, and he thought he was ready to retire after having been what he dubbed a "serial entrepreneur."

On the first Monday after his retirement began, his sons went off to school, his wife went to work, and he was left alone in the house with his 95-year-old mother-in-law. After 2 days, he said, "This is not for me. I have been a player. Suddenly I feel old and redundant." He remembered Candy, a woman who worked at one of the state's Department of Labor career centers and periodically wrote articles for his newspapers. Although he didn't know her well, Justin called her, saying, "I am miserable. Please find something, anything, for me to do." She referred him to a summer job as assistant to a park ranger. He took the job and made the most of it by assisting the ranger in preparing exhibits and informational material about the park. In addition, he was asked to lead nature walks.

At the end of the summer, he called Candy again and asked, "Now what?" She was so impressed with his spirit and energy that she urged him to come to work for the Department of Labor. His assignment was to reorganize their office and procedures. He agreed, as long as he could have Fridays off to ski with his sons. He also needed time to continue writing a coffee table book on the history of his region. He acknowledged Candy's help as follows:

> Without Candy, my late-life benefactor, I would be sitting home feeling sorry for myself. How wonderful in later years to feel you're making a contribution. Most of my friends and fellow graduates from college are only marginally happily retired. And, by the way, I have recently been inducted into the Skiing Hall of Fame.

I found Justin's story so instructive that I asked Mark Savickas, a faculty member at Northeastern Ohio

University College of Medicine, to analyze the case from a narrative perspective. Savickas identified the key themes of Justin's life as the need for movement—both mental and physical:

> As a serial entrepreneur, Justin always had to be on the move. At his essence, he is movement, a man in motion. When he retired, he became frightened because he stopped moving. He had always been a player, meaning a gamesman who knew the score and liked competition, and he often won. The theme of his life continues to be engagement. What mattered was to move toward excitement. This started in adolescence and never stops. When he stopped moving, he felt old and redundant. The only solution was to reactivate his briefly interrupted theme of moving and playing the game. He has been and remains "Maverick: A Man in Motion" or "Maverick: A Man on the Move."[4]

As I was writing this book, I thought about someone for whom I had served as a connector. Elly complained that her husband, Dale, a retired musician, did not have enough to occupy his time. It seemed logical to connect Dale to the Senior Academy, an Elderhostel educational center that offers courses taught by retirees for other retirees. I convinced Dale to come with me to a curriculum committee meeting to discuss the possibility of his teaching a music course. The deal was made, and he taught the course twice. Elly was thrilled that Dale was using his skills in a new way and not just hanging around the house. Although Dale taught the course only twice, he connected to other musicians and music teachers in the area. It opened new opportunities for him.

I started joking to people about how I now saw the need for a new business—Nag Dot Com. I would offer my services to men and women as the person who would nag their partners or spouses. Someone heard about it and called me to see if I would nag her husband. I explained that it was a joke, but it resonated with how many partners feel.

Create New Communities

It is important to identify or create communities that will substitute for work communities. Many retirees wonder, "Where will I go every day? I miss no longer having an office, a place to go that is not home, or a community of like-minded people." It is easier to identify the loss of community than to figure out how to replace the loss. Some retirees hang out at coffee shops with wireless connections; one woman advertised for shared office space on Craig's List; another used the library.

In addition, I have been struck by the number of grassroots support groups that continue to spring up all over the country. As you read the examples below—and these are only the tip of the iceberg— think whether there is some group you can join. If none seems available, consider starting one. Those who participate in these groups find energy and once again begin to feel they matter.

Let's start with Sol, a government employee, who missed the camaraderie of the workplace. Soon after he retired, he decided to start a group of recently retired men and women, mostly from government and academe. They named themselves the Same Boat Group because they were all in the same boat—struggling with adjustment to a new life. Activities in their monthly meetings vary. Sometimes they meet at someone's house or apartment to share experiences; other times, they go on field trips to offbeat places.

Sol's motivation for creating the group stemmed from observing his father, who retired at age 57 and lived until he was 88. During those 31 years, his father did little more than read the paper and become more and more depressed. Sol realized how important it was to build a community of friends after retirement. One group member described the larger group like this: "There is a noncompete clause. We maintain privacy, give each other support, share mutual interests, and have fun. We find it a substitute for work." The Same Boat Group has played an important part in their lives. In fact, it spawned two other groups: a weekly lunch group for whoever wants to come and a "lunch bunch" group of wives of the men in the group.

I've encountered many men who have found community in lunch groups made up of people from the same professional field or with a common interest. One example is Morris, a retired newspaper editor, who enjoyed participating in a men's monthly lunch group called ROMEO, for Retired Old Men Eating Out. Coincidentally, there are ROMEO groups in many cities. The one for retired psychologists provides a forum for the participants to "discuss, decry, moan, and hope for the future of psychology." Another group, the Wise Men, includes men who had been a university president, a reporter, a school superintendent, a newspaper editor, a State Department official, and a lawyer. That group discusses politics, politics, and more politics at their monthly lunches.

I asked Mick, a retired clinical psychologist, how he spent his time. He told me that when he first retired, he was offered opportunities to write books in his field. He refused because he wanted to strike out in new directions rather than continue with his former profession. Then he was invited to join a men's bimonthly breakfast group. The members include entrepreneurs, accountants, doctors, lawyers, and librarians. Mick enjoys the exposure to these different perspectives and likes the fact that their meetings are structured. Each person presents a discussion topic; past topics include the most advantageous ways to leave money to your children, the dynamics of suicide, mergers and acquisitions, and collecting. Attending these bimonthly breakfast meetings provides these men an opportunity to explore, discuss, and learn about issues different from the ones they had worked on professionally. The restaurant where they meet serves as a substitute for Mick's office. He goes there even on days they are not meeting—just to hang out, see people, read the paper, and feel connected to the world.

In the same way, women create community by participating in a wide variety of clubs and organizations, including networking groups like the International Women's Forum, made up of community leaders, and monthly support groups where members discuss personal issues. One of the latter, called Women in Their Fifties in the Eighties, started in the early 1980s but is still meeting regularly. They discuss the challenges they face, such as being a mother-in-law, the meaning of friendship, when to lie, the importance of giving praise, resilience, and taking risks.

Bernice Bratter and Helen Dennis started Project Renewment for women to share strategies that would help them recharge as they carved out new paths. Their book, *Project Renewment: The First Retirement Model for Career Women*, provides guidelines for forming such a group.[5]

Another group, the Red Hat Society, numbers more than 1 million members who can be easily identified by their red hats and purple accessories. The society was started several years ago as a way to have fun, enjoy life, and bond. The musical about the Red Hat Society, *Hats! A New Musical for the Rest of Your Life*, reflects the message, "We matter. We are not invisible. We are not has-beens."[6] They have created a visible community that connects them to others, not only in their immediate city but nationwide. (You can see how to join an existing society or create a new chapter by visiting http://www.redhatsociety.org.)

Move to a New Community

Moving to a retirement or continuing care living situation is a way to build new relationships, overcome loneliness, and ensure that you will be part of a community. According to a survey, *The Future of Retirement Living*, 86% of preretirees indicated that they would prefer to live independently in their own homes after retiring. Their second choice would be a move to an adult retirement community.[7] The choices are complex as people weigh the options; in addition to staying in place, these could include moving to a condo, active adult community, independent living community, continuing care retirement community, naturally occurring retirement community, or intentional community.

Emily, a member of the Women's Retirement Seminar, agonized over whether to move to a retirement community. Her husband had died a year previously, leaving her unsettled about living alone. Although she was still working part time at a government agency, she knew that full-time retirement was in the near future. She was afraid that once she retired, living in her big house could be isolating. Another woman in the group announced that she was signing papers that day to finalize her move into a retirement community, which she was doing for the same reason—to find community. Depressed and frightened, the second woman sighed, "I will make it by just breathing in and out." Both women felt that without husbands, they had lost their social capital and that to regain some of it, they needed to move to a ready-made community.

The group discussed the pros and cons of moving into such a community. Emily explained her dilemma:

> You have to be ready to define yourself as "old." You see some people on walkers, and they seem much older than you are. In addition, it forces you to think that this is the last stop before the end. And you resent some of the regimentation.

For many, though, the positives of moving into a ready-made community outweigh the negatives. Once in a community, residents are, for the most part, enthusiastic. In one community, the residents talked about the men's lunch table and the women's lunch table. "Whenever I feel lonely, I can find someone to be with." Another woman said, "I will always have a home here, no matter what happens to me. I feel secure, and my children don't have to worry about me."

What happens to those living in planned communities who fall between the cracks, who do not feel they belong to the community, who feel ignored and marginal? There are some projects underway that have the potential for ensuring that residents feel included and that they matter. One such program (briefly described in chap. 1 of this volume), Masterpiece Living: An Experiment in Successful Aging, was developed through a collaboration between the MacArthur Foundation Research Network on Aging (an interdisciplinary team of scholars to study the positive aspects of aging) and the Westport Advisors (an organization that operates retirement communities). Their charge is to "create a living environment that facilitates, encourages, and motivates behavior patterns . . . [that are] associated with successful aging."[8]

Among the many initiatives they instituted, one of the most important was the introduction of a lifestyle coordinator staff position. I visited a retirement community, the Sarasota Bay Club in Sarasota, Florida, and met with the lifestyle coordinator. She works on a personalized living plan for each resident, which covers the resident's physical, mental, social, and spiritual life.

ENERGIZE YOUR CONTINUING RELATIONSHIPS

There are many ways to meet new people and connect with new activities, all of which will maintain and increase your social capital. But engaging in new activities with new people is only half of the story. Retirement provides the opportunity to energize and improve your existing relationships. You might now have time to deepen your relationships with family and friends. The changes could be for better or for worse, but as is generally true at any time in your life, change brings both rewards and the stress of adjustment.

In my conversations with retirees, here are some of the things I have heard them say about their changed relationships with family:

- "I used to have my own home office. Now we share an office and a computer."
- "My husband keeps interrupting me, asking where I am going and when I will be back."

- "I seem to be a permanent babysitter for my grand-children" or, alternatively, "I never get to see my grandchildren. They live too far away."

Change the Ground Rules With Spouses and Partners

I asked the members of the Same Boat Group how re-tirement affected their marriages. One man reported a conflict over the dog: "My wife insists that I walk it, but calls it her dog and has it sleep on her side of the bed. Whose dog is it? Before I retired, I had no time to walk the dog."

Some couples respond to the stress of more togeth-erness by separating or divorcing. But most others ne-gotiate, set boundaries, and stay together. Paul and Martin are an example of a couple who successfully navigated a rocky transition. Paul, a college administra-tor, was offered a buyout that was too good to turn down. They decided to use this opportunity to move from Chicago to California. They wanted a warmer cli-mate and figured that because Martin was an office manager, he could always find a job while Paul figured out what to do with his new-found time. In California, Martin found a job immediately, but Paul became dis-couraged and depressed when he couldn't seem to find anything appropriate to do.

Martin spent the day out of the house working, and Paul's day consisted of watching TV, cleaning house, and doing errands. When Martin returned home, tired and ready for a quiet dinner, Paul wanted to go out and do something. Martin began getting irritated with Paul's lack of understanding of the time demands on him; Paul felt that Martin was not sympathetic and was pulling away from their relationship. For a while, it seemed, their relationship was in trouble.

Paul finally took an important step by asking his pastor what he could do to get involved in his new community. The pastor asked Paul to do some volunteer administrative work in the church. After a few months, Paul took on the major challenge of revamping the computer system. He is now working part time in a paid position. Fortunately, Paul's strategy of reaching out and the responsiveness of the pastor saved his relationship with Martin. The lesson they want to teach others: Don't give up, don't nag each other, coach each other, and stay committed to the relationship.

In another instance of a couple out of sync, Cyn described the problems that she and her husband were experiencing. When they both were working, they couldn't wait to retire. They were in total agreement about the path they would take. When the time came, they sold most of their furniture, art, and other possessions and cruised on their boat for 5 years. To Syd, this was the beginning of an easy retirement. Subsequently, at Cyn's urging, they sold the boat and moved back to land. Cyn saw this as her opportunity to continue adventuring—by changing careers and starting something entirely new. She got a job as director of an artists' retreat. Syd chose a looser path and each evening waited for her to come home so they could do something together. He expected to continue on this path with little structure to guide him. She expected to continue working. She does not want to give up her role in the arts but feels guilty about Syd waiting aimlessly for her to return from work. Deciding that they had to overcome this impasse, they agreed to go to a couples counselor to work on goals that would be good for them individually and as a couple.

Despite some of the experiences recounted here, it's important to realize that not everyone's retirement experience is negative, lonely, or sad. One man wrote on his retirement blog that he was angry with those who write only about the problems of retirement. "I wish that someone could witness and then report on the delight I and my wife experience now that we can spend all our time together," he reported. "I would like to see more even-handed discussions about retirement—not just the negative."

Now, About Sex

Willa Bernhard, the sex therapist mentioned in chapter 1, studied 50 women between 60 and 90 to uncover their attitudes and practices regarding sex.[9] She found that interest and desire levels varied. There were women, particularly in their 60s and early 70s, who enjoyed sex, but there were many of all ages who were no longer interested in sex. Most women who were married or in a relationship continued to have sex if their partners were interested, but many said they preferred sex that didn't end with intercourse. Some women without a partner or whose partner had no sexual desire were comfortable pleasuring themselves, according to Bernhard.

Married women's interest in sex varied widely. Some were still enjoying a sexual relationship with their husbands, others had sex to satisfy their husbands, and still others had to adapt to disabilities of their husbands' that affected lovemaking. The women who enjoyed sex the most were in new love relationships. All of the women in Bernhard's study said that a partner's caring and sensitivity were the prerequisites to sexual desire, indicating that the key to a successful sex life for women follows from a successful relationship with a partner who is loving, sensitive, and responsive. Bernhard commented to me that "communication between people becomes foreplay."[10] Meaningful sex can take forms other than intercourse. Partners often are shy and embarrassed about discussing what gives them sexual gratification, especially if what was once enjoyable is no longer so. And many who speak openly report that warmth and intimacy are the major factors in their sex lives.

Bernhard did not prescribe one sexual path over another. Instead, she suggested an exchange between couples in which they share their needs and expectations with one another. This process can stimulate a couple's lovemaking. For some, discussing sexual matters might be awkward, but it is better than living with the elephant in the room.

117

Make Time for Family

You may recall the story about Ruth in chapter 3. She was the former executive director of a nonprofit organization who was forced into an early retirement. She made the transition from an extremely demanding job after spending a week at a meditation retreat. After the retreat, she began to see her new life situation as an opportunity to renew family relationships. Although she and her mother lived in the same community, Ruth previously had had little time to spend with her. After retirement, she spent at least a day a week with her mother. They went on shopping sprees, had lunch, met mutual friends, and generally had fun.

For 10 years, Ruth had never taken time to visit her sister, who lives across the state. After retirement, she began visiting her on a regular basis. They regained some of their former closeness and arranged to meet every few weeks.

One retired couple told me about a week-long vacation at a beach resort they took with their adult children and spouses and their grandchildren. During the week, some old tensions emerged—sibling disagreements, concern over how the retired grandparents were handling their lives, tensions between one of the couples about how to control their small children, and stress about money.

One of the adult children decided to change the dynamics. She suggested a memory game. At dinner, each person was asked to recall a positive or humorous story from the past. The tensions seemed to disappear as memories of positive connections took over. The week ended as a happy, uplifting experience. Family reunions and vacations will not always turn out that way, but it is important to make time to be together in neutral territory as a way to unify the family.

Use the Internet

Current and future generations of retirees have an incredibly effective tool for energizing relationships: the Internet. At a bargain price, it offers a number of ways to stay in touch with friends and family, including e-mailing news and photos, instant messaging, family Web pages, and blogging. Blogging in particular has been a lifesaver for some, who say that it makes them feel connected to other people.

If you didn't master Internet basics when you were working, when you retire you'll have plenty of time to develop the skills required to stay in touch with your friends and family. Community colleges and a wide range of organizations—or even your children—can be a big help in teaching you. Even if you don't have your own computer, you can probably get free access to one at your local library.

One retirement community has designated one of the public rooms as "Your Internet Space." They provide the winning combination of free lessons and available computers.

Find Ways to Overcome Loneliness

Mary S. Furlong, author of *Turning Silver Into Gold: How to Profit in the New Boomer Marketplace*, reported that almost "a third of women age 65 to 74 and 57% of those over age 85 live alone."[11] Of course, many are happy, choosing to live alone. But many find coping with loneliness a major issue. The Retirement Seminar Group that I refer to throughout this book was originally formed as a way for members to support each other during their postretirement years. Over time, the focus of the group changed from dealing with retirement to dealing with issues of aging. The group members decided to spend one session discussing loneliness.

Most of the women in the group were either divorced or widowed. They said it was hard to have no one to react to your thoughts, no one with whom to discuss the news, and no one to care whether you got home on time or "to talk trivia with." They were struggling to find ways to replace the social contact of a life companion with friends or even another partner.

One woman valued having several kinds of friends: a confidante with whom to discuss her innermost thoughts, friends to discuss what was going on in her life and share mutual interests and concerns, and acquaintances. Her strategy was, "If I feel lonely, I call someone, reach out." Others had moved to retirement communities where there was "immediate human contact" or had taken on new jobs or returned to old ones. One woman advised, "Don't be shy about joining couples or even initiating activities with couples. Just re-define yourself as a 'unicycle' instead of a 'fifth wheel.' "

Fun and Friends—Best Buffers to Stress

Author Shelley E. Taylor concluded that many women are good at caring and friendship because they have an instinct to do so. The title of her book *The Tending Instinct: Women, Men, and the Biology of Our Relationships*, reflects this hypothesis. This poses a friendship conundrum: We know friendship is critical to our well-being; yet we often push it to the back burner because of the demands of work and family.[12]

Author and sociologist Lillian Rubin pointed out that friends are very much a part of our convoy—they are our cobiographers:

> Friends . . . provide a reference outside the family against which to measure and judge ourselves; who help us during passages that require our separation and individuation; who support us as we adapt to new roles and new rules; who heal the hurts and make good the deficits of other relationships in our lives; who offer the place and encouragement for the development of parts of self that, for whatever reasons, are inaccessible in the family context. It's with friends that we test our sense . . . of the possibilities of a self-yet-to-become.[13]

Many of us attend reunions or look up old friends as a way to remember our past, to compare notes on the various ways our lives have unfolded, and to reconnect with others who "knew me when." Continuity with your past adds to your sense of stability. For example,

Norma decided to go to her high school reunion. She loved reminiscing, comparing herself with others in terms of who looked better, and enjoying the comradeship with her former classmates. After that, she arranged for regular get-togethers with six of her high school friends, going off to a spa at least once a year. They laugh, relax, and share their reactions to life's ups and downs.

Aina Segal, a therapist, felt a pang of nostalgia when she heard her friend Norma talk about renewing friendships. Aina described her escape from Latvia and the time she and her mother spent in refugee camps in her touching memoir about tragedy and resilience, *Battered Heart*. She had no childhood friends to visit, no reunions to attend, no available past to provide a sense of continuity—something we all need. Her friends from early life remained suspended in time. She knew them only as children, whereas Norma could see her friends age as she was aging. Aina recognized her loss, mourned for it, and moved on.[14]

Another group, mostly boomers, mostly married, use monthly dinners as a way to let off steam and complain to others they can trust. One woman expressed her anger at her husband, who felt he was in charge of all their decisions—including where they would retire. Another shared her concerns about her changing friendship with someone she had considered her "best buddy." In general, their discussions focused on relationships and what they wanted for themselves for the rest of their lives.

Julie, herself a full-time worker with a retired husband, a college-age son, and aging parents decided to create a fun experience, bond with other women, and make friends—a high priority. Her idea was to plan a party to celebrate being 65. Some of her friends had retired, others were looking for retirement careers, and many were continuing to balance work and family but beginning to think of a future without paid work. She started discussing the party with a core group of women, then added other women along the way, many of whom she knew only casually. They met monthly for 6 months. The process of planning the party was uplifting and brought unexpected benefits. One member of the group was overwhelmed by caring for her mother, who had Alzheimer's and required a great deal of attention. She was in a quandary about what arrangements to make for her. She commented, "Planning this party, meeting other women, and having fun is a lifesaver."

The party was a great success. Their program included "Boomer Cheers" in which they made fun of themselves getting older. There was music, dancing, and joking, and each table was covered with M&Ms with "Viagra" printed on them. The party was so invigorating, Julie reported, that "my girl group got back together this week to affirm we will do another boomer party with the theme 'Boomers Do Disco.' "

This group rediscovered what we all know—that fun and friends are a winning combination. Julie understood that the time and energy it took to plan this party brought real benefits; she had read and seen ample evidence that women's friendships increase longevity, alleviate stress, and help them improve their lives.

Conclusion

Psychiatrist Gene Cohen found that the key to a successful retirement is feeling in control (*mastery*) and having meaningful engagements. Unfortunately, many retirees with busy social lives still feel unfulfilled. Most people, Cohen suggested, need individual as well as group activities, some that require high energy and mobility—like dancing and travel—and others that require low energy and low mobility—such as writing, reading, and listening to music.[15] As you think about your own retirement, think about engaging in group as well as solitary activities and in a mix of high-energy and low-energy activities.

Many of those I interviewed who paid attention to Cohen's advice by maintaining a balance of intimate and community relationships and combining low- and high-energy activities expressed feelings of satisfaction. To revitalize your relationships, reframe retirement as an opportunity to make new contacts, seize the opportunity of having more time to reconnect with family and friends, and brainstorm ways to live your life so that you have plenty of social capital in the bank.

It's Your Turn: Tips on How to Reshape Your Relationships

Here are some winning strategies others have used to reshape their relationships. The following tips can stimulate your thinking about ways to energize your existing relationships and create new ones:

1. Assess Your Relationships

Think of your relationships as consisting of three circles, and imagine yourself in the center circle. Those closest to you are in the second circle, and the third circle contains acquaintances and work relationships. Imagine your circle, and then ask yourself, Do you need one, two, or more closest friends? Do you need a large group of acquaintances, many of whom were related to your work? What will you substitute for these acquaintances once your work ends?

2. Make Connections

Overall, do you feel satisfied with your relationships? If not, think about how you can begin to connect to a new community or to friends with whom you've lost touch. Will you use acquaintances to help connect you? How will you network with others? Make a long-term plan of what you really want to happen. Then break it down into manageable activities, and make a short-term plan that is reasonable.

3. Start Your Own Support Group

Start a Project Renewment Group, a Red Hat Society chapter, or a book or lunch club.

4. Initiate an Expectation Exchange

Overall, do you feel satisfied with your close personal relationships? Work on your changing relationships and routines. If you are living with someone, talk over your expectations with him or her. Discuss such topics as whether the time has come to retire, where to retire, and the amount and kind of sexual activity you enjoy. The ability to fully discuss, negotiate, and compromise on an issue that is important to you can be helpful in both resolving the issue and strengthening the relationship. If you have difficulty finding a resolution, consider meeting with a neutral party, attending a couples seminar on negotiation, or seeking professional help. It's all about negotiation and setting boundaries.

5. Support Your Partner's Dream

Sometimes the individuals in a couple have dreams that are not in sync. It is important to know your partner's dream and to support it if you can.

5

Revitalize Your Purpose

Ava, an exercise therapist, kept reading that boomers were going to change the face of retirement. About to retire, she felt totally inadequate. She did not see herself as a boomer trendsetter. Rather, she saw herself as someone searching for a new purpose. What advice could I offer?

I am reminded of an apocryphal story of a cowpoke consoling a young woman who had just missed the stagecoach that was supposed to take her out to California, where she and her dashing cavalry officer fiancé were to be married. As she sobbed, he comforted her, "Don't worry, Missy. There'll be another stage a'-comin' along next week."

I pass his message along to people in transition, especially those facing the challenge of reshaping their purpose when they leave their main career path. The message? Even when things look confusing and dark, there are other doors to open and other stagecoaches on the way. And while you are waiting for one to come along, figure out your passion and then choose your path. Even if that passion has been burning unfulfilled for 30, 40, or 50 years or more, retirement offers you many more chances to live a fulfilling life.

IDENTIFY YOUR PASSION—SELECT YOUR FOCUS

Ask yourself, What do I wish I had done with my life? Is there still time to build that into my future? What do I regret that I have left undone? Once you've analyzed your regrets, turn them into a new focus. For example, Neil, a writer, regretted never learning to play the piano. For his 50th birthday, he bought a piano, took lessons, and wrote a memoir for his family about his experiences. This proved good practice for his hoped-for early retirement.

Sometimes it is difficult to find an activity that fits well with your skills and schedule. That is where friends, family, career counselors, psychologists, coaches, social workers, and other professionals can help. However, the person needing help needs to be ready to ask for help, willing to try several avenues if one does not work out, and able to implement plans that seem reasonable.

In the course of interviewing people for my work on retirement, I met Millie, a warm, nurturing woman with an eighth-grade education. She had worked as a baby practical nurse. Between jobs, she would revisit families she had worked for and give them a hand. In this way, she kept in touch with the children she had nursed. As a result of diabetes, Millie's leg was amputated. Without the financial resources to pay for the kind of help and equipment she would need to become active, she became a shut-in. She was depressed.

However, Millie's strength was her willingness to ask for help. She remembered Elinor, a career counselor she'd worked for years before. Millie called her and explained how miserable she was—that she had no outlet for her nurturing. Realizing that Millie was housebound, Elinor arranged with the social worker at a nearby hospital to give Millie a list of all the patients who were discharged each week. Her job was to make a phone call a few days after they were released to check on how they were doing. This provided people with needed support in the transition from hospital to home. Millie felt her life had been saved—and it had. But she saved it by reaching out for help. Luckily, when she reached out, she found the right person.

I have said this frequently, but I want to emphasize it once more: Retiring is like graduating from high school or college. Many graduates need help in planning their next steps. Some need career counseling, others coaching, and others therapy. If you're floundering, it is critical to acknowledge that you need help and to search for it.

A useful way to start revitalizing your purpose is to ask yourself, "Do I want to focus on creativity, learning, working, volunteering, or kinkeeping?" I describe these focus areas in the following sections.

Creative Focus

Psychologist and author Gene D. Cohen studied the possibilities for the creative spirit to emerge as one ages. Research on the aging brain documents that with age, the "creative push" is not only possible but probable. In addition, retirement can provide the time needed to pursue creative endeavors. As an added benefit, he found, retirees who participated actively in the arts needed fewer doctor visits. In other words, creative endeavors result in positive payoffs. Cohen clarified that anyone can be creative if, by *creativity*, you mean a fresh perspective, a new idea, or participation in any of the arts as an amateur.[1]

Emeritus Rabbi Harold S. Silver is an example of someone for whom creativity became a main retirement focus. At first, backing away from his full-time responsibilities as a rabbi caused him some concern. But over time, he found new purpose in his life by becoming an accomplished stone sculptor.

This hobby began when he and his wife started spending some winter months on Longboat Key, Florida, and a friend cajoled him into taking a beginning stone sculpture course at the local art center. He became immersed, and on returning to Hartford, Connecticut, where he spent most of his time, he continued studying with a tutor. At the time I interviewed him, Rabbi Silver had created 11 different 60- to 70-pound works in alabaster, limestone, and marble, all on Biblical themes. This hobby is a logical continuation of his past because of the Biblical focus and his early appreciation of the arts.

"At this point," he wrote to me, "my mood is not to sell a single piece. As a newcomer, I love them all. Each piece is like my own 'child,' and how can one dispose of one's kids?" He was surprised and delighted when his work was recognized by the faculty at the art center where he studied.

Because Rabbi Silver made such an excellent adjustment to retirement, I asked him to share some words of wisdom that could benefit others. He suggested the following:

- Find your own space, if possible. "I built a very attractive retirement study where I continue my correspondence and phoning."
- Diversify your activities. "In addition to sculpting, I now spend more time with family; narrate talking books for the blind; and serve as an elder statesman to my successors, their assistants, and members of the congregation."
- Respond to invitations, and take advantage of "happenstance."
- Maintain relationships with former colleagues, but do not burden them; renew contacts with others who have already enriched your life.
- Venture into new creative activities with a rebalance of work, love, and play.

In sum, Rabbi Silver developed his creative side while maintaining his religious and spiritual focus. His new artistic activity provided tremendous excitement and pleasure, enabling him to experience his new role as rabbi emeritus with satisfaction, not despair.

Learning Focus

I found that many people identified their passion through learning. The growth in the number and type of educational opportunities for older retirees testifies to the rewards that many retirees find in "going back to school." Most of these opportunities are noncredit adult education programs, although it's not unheard of for a retiree to study for a degree. Universities, 4-year colleges, community colleges, and local school boards also offer noncredit programs. All predictions point to the continued growth of universities in the business of adult education. Whatever the structure, the basic principles are similar: Retirees are offered noncredit courses that interest them, often at a very low fee. Afterward, many become peer teachers themselves in the program.

A model program, the North Carolina Center for Creative Retirement, was established in 1988 as an integral part of the University of North Carolina in Asheville, and the program has received many awards. It is designed to promote lifelong learning in addition to leadership and service opportunities for retirees. Dave and his wife retired to Asheville when they were in their early 60s so that they could become a part of the center and take volunteer leadership roles there and in the community. The model of a center as part of a university or community college is growing in many communities.

Paul, a retired senior science reporter, said in response to my question about what advice he would give to prospective retirees, "Keep learning and have a hobby." In his career, he reported on cutting-edge issues. His profession required him to study a body of information, distill it, and write about it in terms a layperson could understand—all in a very short period of time. His adrenalin was always rushing. I asked if he had had a letdown, maybe even some depression, after retiring.

He denied such feelings for two reasons: First, his news service kept asking him to write important articles on an ad hoc basis, and second, he had become a learner: "I used to work on present and future issues; now I am studying the past. I read books about American history." Paul has combined adventure travel and learning. In fact, he and his wife were out of their hometown more than 150 days last year, visiting Antarctica, Africa, and other parts of the world.

I asked Paul to go into more detail about his passion for learning and travel. He shared the following with me:

How can anybody not be a learner? With just a teaspoon of curiosity, a person is compelled to seek new knowledge through the Internet, through libraries filled with fascinating books, and from the increasingly excellent channels of learning on television. For everyone, no matter what his or her academic background, there is an immense, untapped universe of information waiting to be explored.

133

For instance, I read extensively about Darwin, his voyage of discovery, and the reluctant acceptance by science of the principles of evolution. Some in society are still fighting the idea. But that called for a trip to the Galapagos Islands, and we saw firsthand what so fascinated Darwin.

Fascinated by changes in the global climate, my wife and I for years have traveled to destinations where we could study the effects of the changes. These have included Churchill, Canada, to observe the Hudson Bay bear colony, the group that is most immediately affected by a warming Earth, and East Africa, where an increasing human population is pushing into lands once the home of lion, elephant, leopard, and rhino.

Clearly, learning serves many purposes. It is a connecting link to others; it can be a substitute for work activities and, perhaps most important, a way to stretch your mind.

Working Focus

Increasingly, the reality of retirement includes working in some form. In 2001, the AARP conducted a nationwide survey of workers between the ages of 50 and 70. The majority planned to work past retirement age—some for money, some to cover health insurance, some for fun, some to feel useful. Some "retirees" planned to move from full-time to part-time work, others to change jobs, and some to start their own businesses. Currently, of "retirees" working after retirement, about half are in jobs different from their preretirement careers.[2] You might ask why this is considered retirement. As mentioned in the Introduction chapter in this book, it can be a career change that takes place after your main career or job. Often, those changing careers take new jobs without benefits because they are receiving either Social Security or a pension from their previous work.

In addition to civic engagement, boomers are experimenting with new ways to make money. This entrepreneurial urge strikes many who have worked as employees in the government, postal service, education, or the nonprofit sector. Author Mary S. Furlong provided a "tool kit" for helping boomers become successful entrepreneurs.[3]

I learned about Jake, who is an example of a boomer turned entrepreneur. After retiring from a government job, boredom set in. By surfing the Internet, he discovered the world of franchises, and after several months of serious study, he bought a pet care franchise. He is not alone; many people 55 and older are purchasing franchises. Jeff Elgin is the CEO of FranChoice Inc., a company that provides free consulting to consumers looking for a franchise that best matches their needs. Others seek career counselors to help them figure out their next career or, as Marc Freedman, founder of the civic engagement movement called it, their "encore career."[4]

Although the percentages differ, many surveys have confirmed that baby boomers include some kind of work in their plans for retirement. A study of postretirement workers by Merrill Lynch[5] found that only 6% were working full time; the rest were working part time, often in what is called *phased retirement*, in which the employee remains with the same employer but reduces the number of work hours or days. Higher education institutions have been leaders in developing phased retirement for their faculty and staff.

Phased retirement was the approach I took in my own retirement. When I announced that I planned to retire, the University of Maryland suggested I reduce my activities gradually. I stopped teaching but continued running the center I was directing. This arrangement enabled me to begin living a life without teaching and advising but to stay connected to the university.

In the past, many private companies have shied away from offering phased retirement to their employees because they believed that federal law prevented them from paying an employee a pension and a salary at the same time. The law has changed recently, and employers are creating more and more phased retirement opportunities for their staff.

Harry, another person interviewed for this book, is an example of a retiree working part time in a new endeavor. He had been a butcher in a meat factory earning a decent living. Fifteen years after retirement, he had a new job—driving older people to and from doctors' appointments and airports. Both the work and the money were rewarding to him. But this definitely was not the life he'd imagined before retiring. For 15 years, his Social Security and savings had enabled him to fish; play some golf; work out at a gym; learn bridge; and, as he said, "live the good life." Then one day, he woke up to reality. Blessed with an excellent physical condition, he realized that he might outlive his money. The idea of creating the driving business emerged from conversations with friends who knew he did not want to work at a desk or any type of "inside" job. His story has a happy ending: Harry loves his work and sees it as a wonderful career change.

Volunteering Focus

Volunteering can be a critical outlet for everyone, but especially for retirees. According to psychologist Dan P. McAdams and his colleagues, it taps into their need to leave their mark (*agency*) and connect with others (*communion*). *Agency* refers to the desire to keep expanding and asserting oneself, to "defy death by constructing legacies that live on."[6] For some, immortality is achieved by replacing themselves with something tangible. Think of all the scholarships, buildings, and books that bear people's names as a way for them to live on. Volunteering also enables *communion*, or connection with others, "to care for that which one has created . . . until it is ready to be on its own."[7] For many retirees, volunteering is a way to underscore their presence as they replace the routines, social contacts, and purpose they lost by retiring from a job. According to developmental psychologist Erik Erikson, a person who stays vitally involved in life (he called such people *generative*) avoids feeling stagnant, burned out, or used up.[8]

There are several avenues to follow as you prepare for meaningful work or volunteer activities, including conferences, certificate programs, or workshops. One example is the Legacy Leadership Program at the University of Maryland's School of Public Health. The program was designed to accomplish what Marc Freedman proposed—to be a conduit for active retirees to become engaged in civic activities. The Legacy Leadership Institutes combine lifelong learning and civic engagement for Maryland residents over 50 (for information about individual institutes, see the Legacy Leadership Program's Web site: http://www.sph.umd.edu/hlsa/AGING/lli_general.cfm).

Ann is an example of a satisfied participant in the Legacy Leadership Program. After retirement, she felt that something was missing. A "digger" who is always looking for opportunities, she participated in the university's Legacy Leadership Institutes program, and later she was placed as a part-time volunteer in the office of a U.S. senator. She attributed her success in locating a meaningful volunteer job to the Legacy program.

There's no question that there are many important roles for volunteers in American society. But sometimes retirees find it hard to encounter exactly the right match—an activity that both fits well with their skills and schedule and gives them personal satisfaction. In addition, the volunteer activities that provide most satisfaction are those that have continuity. Marta, a member of the Same Boat Group described in chapter 4 of this volume, complained that her volunteer activities helping nonprofits advertise their big fundraising events required her to move from organization to organization on an as-needed basis. She pointed out that as a "serial" volunteer, her activities changed periodically, resulting in what she called "transitory mattering." When each volunteer activity ended, once again it was like facing retirement day. She claimed, "With each volunteer activity, I experience endings and beginnings. I am always thinking, what do I want to do next?"

Others echo Marta's experience. For example, when MaryAnn retired from teaching, she found that her pension was enough to enable her to volunteer, and she looked forward to finding interesting opportunities. Every place she contacted wanted her to address envelopes; make photocopies; or do what was, to her, boring office work. She had always dreamed of working on a newspaper but knew that at her age, without experience, she was not likely to qualify for writing and reporting tasks. At the suggestion of a counselor, MaryAnn decided to set up an internship for herself. She approached the managing editor of the local newspaper and offered to serve as an intern for 6 months. They set up a rotation for her so that she could volunteer in different departments.

At the end of her self-made internship, they asked her to stay and help in a permanent volunteer job, circulating among the departments as needed. She loved the variety and being part of a community. She realized that what she had missed was belonging to a permanent group. MaryAnn said, "I wish there were internship programs for retirees. I had to figure this out for myself, but everyone needs opportunities for meaningful volunteering."

Kinkeeping Focus

Kinkeeping is a term sociologists use to describe maintaining family and interpersonal relationships. For many, retirement provides the time to arrange family gatherings and reunions. It also implies something else—the possibility of assuming a caregiver role with kin.

Caregiving is a double-edged sword. On one hand, it provides an outlet for our need to nurture and to be generative by caring for the next or the previous generation. According to psychologist Shelley E. Taylor, it provides opportunities to express one's need to care for others: "My work suggests . . . that the human response to stress is characterized at least as much by tending to and befriending others, a pattern that is especially true of women."[9] This observation is underscored in McAdams and de St. Aubin's edited book *Generativity and Adult Development: How and Why We Care for the Next Generation*.[10] The chapters examine generativity (the concept first described by Erikson, as mentioned earlier). The need to care for others is part and parcel of progressing through the life span. It may take different forms and be motivated by different forces, but resolving it positively leads to well-being and happiness.

On the other hand, caregivers often feel overwhelmed and frantic, feeling pulled in too many directions. For example, middle-aged individuals and couples caring for both adolescent children and elderly parents (and who are also often at the peak of their careers) can feel stretched because their parents or adult children depend too much on them. In fact, a growing group of middle-aged people at the top of their careers are taking a break and moving close to their parents when their parents are in failing health. Grandparents providing primary caregiving for grandchildren face the paradoxical situation of feeling that they matter too much, but most would not have it any other way. It is therefore possible to matter too much or too little. It's hard to get it just right, but it's worth the effort.

Caregiving becomes a major issue in midlife. A group of baby boomers I interviewed for the PBS special *Retire Smart, Retire Happy*[11] expressed two major concerns: Would they outlive their money, and would they be able to emotionally and financially handle probable caregiving responsibilities? It is fair to say that most baby boomers and older individuals will at some time in their lives become caregivers for a family member. This is an enormous challenge and can require a total rearrangement of resources. Judy, a retired educator, and her husband took her 3-year-old grandson in when his mother, their daughter, died of cancer. They cared for their grandson, and when his father remarried, the grandson went to live with his father. Judy had totally rearranged her retirement to care for her grandson, and when he went to live with his father and new stepmother, Judy had mixed emotions—both happy and sad.

A host of colorful, descriptive terms have entered our vocabulary as a result of several demographic trends. Today, it's not unheard of for a 70-year-old daughter, for example, to take care of her 90-year-old mother. Whether we call these caregivers the "sandwich generation" or the "bridge generation" or say they are on the "daughter track" (a later in life version of the "mommy track"), kinkeepers experience the burdens and joys of caregiving that can come from being part of three-, four-, and even five-generation families.

When AARP surveyed boomers' attitudes about caring for their parents, they found that they were providing care willingly and were prepared to help in the future if it became necessary. Take the example of Walter, an interior designer. At age 55, he took early retirement and moved from Seattle, Washington, to Madison, Wisconsin, after realizing that his father, now in a nursing home, needed to have an advocate nearby. Walter did not make the decision to move lightly. He mulled it over for 6 months as he flew back and forth to visit his father.

As a result of discussions with a therapist, who helped him understand his dual motivations—to help his father as well as to alleviate the guilt he felt for not being there—Walter closed his office in Seattle and settled in Madison. Dealing with the ambiguity of his own career being on hold and the unknown of his father's life expectancy was stressful, but Walter found joining a men's group in his church helpful in building his social support network. In addition, he visited Seattle periodically to keep the door open for returning there.

Many retirees find they need to take on the role of kinkeeping when a spouse becomes ill or disabled. The issue of financial resources becomes paramount. Even for those who have the financial resources to hire to assistance, the stress can be overwhelming. One woman, Sandra, shared her concerns with me:

> I feel as if I have gone back in time to when I used to carpool children, take them to doctors, and revolve my life around them. Now I am driving my husband to doctors, almost daily. There is so much that goes into this—picking up prescriptions, arranging coverage when I am unavailable. It is really a tough time in life.

Another woman, Bev, also shared her story:

> I have recovered from my back surgeries 99%. When I get tired, my lower back aches, but not bad. I try not to lift heavy things or bend too much, but that is hard, given that I have a lot of that to do caring for Bud. He has good days and not-so-good days—alas, very exhausting. Where are the good old carefree days we used to have? How did we get to this stage of life, when I still think I'm only about 27? I think your idea about all of us living near each other so we can exchange services is a good idea.

To return to the baby boomer group that was part of the PBS special, *Retire Smart, Retire Happy*,[12] many anticipated a future that might require caregiving for some family member, thus precluding boomers from designing a life for themselves. A case in point: According to 2000 U.S. Census Bureau statistics, more than 3.9 million children under 18—approximately 1 in 12—were living in 2.4 million households headed by grandparents or other relatives.[13] Or to put it another way, there were approximately 2.4 million grandparents taking on primary responsibility for their grandchildren under 18. Many of these grandparents assumed this responsibility because their adult children had died, were on drugs, or were incarcerated.

At the University of Maryland, we initiated a project called Grandparents Raising Grandchildren. We met with groups of low-income grandparents to discover how they handled the complexities of their new role, which included dealing with the school and the welfare systems, and to provide support for them. We found their strengths amazing but understandable in the context of the need to matter. One grandfather said,

> This is not the way I planned my retirement, but I wouldn't have it any other way. They need me, and I will be there for them as long as I live. However, I worry what will happen when I die.

Many kinkeepers find that they need a family therapist, social worker, counselor, physician, or other professional to help them improve their coping strategies and control feelings of guilt. Those receiving care may need this assistance, too; one woman complained that her children were critical of the amount of money she was spending on help for herself because, she believed, they did not want to see their inheritance dwindle.

Most of the women felt that their adult children were concerned and caring, but they said that their children's own family commitments prevented them from helping on a regular basis.

Leisure and Play Focus

We think of *play*—any activity that has no goal other than to have fun—as the province of the young. But many retirees are young at heart and continue to build on the lifelong need to play. George E. Vaillant wrote in his landmark book *Aging Well* that a task of retirement is "learning how to maintain self-respect while letting go of self-importance. . . . What is helpful . . . is being able to play."[14]

Travel, visiting spas, mountain climbing, Outward Bound for the over 60 group, hang gliding like George H. W. Bush, cruising, motorcycling, grandparent–grandchildren camps, bird-watching—all are avenues for leisure and play. M. S. Furlong devoted a chapter of her book, *Turning Silver Into Gold: How to Profit in the New Boomer Marketplace,* to leisure. She pointed out that "Americans over age 50 account for 45% of trips. . . . They consume 80% of all luxury travel . . . take 72% of all RV trips and account for 70% of cruise passengers."[15] In addition, about 20% of all grandparents took a trip with their grandchildren in 2000. Special niche travel groups and agencies abound. Search the Internet, or ask a travel agent for leisure opportunities that suit your interests and pocketbook.

Experiential travel, which includes travel and a stint volunteering for a short time at the destination, is an interesting new twist for boomers. It is not enough to celebrate an occasion; there is often an educational aspect involved. You might visit a golf spa, a tennis camp, or a sailing school. My friend Barbara, newly retired, planned to do something challenging for her 65th birthday. She had been afraid of water all her life, but she decided to join a week-long sailing school. After that experience, she felt she could handle anything.

CHOOSE YOUR RETIREMENT PATH

Now that I have outlined some ways to focus your energies, the next step in reshaping your Purpose is to figure out which path makes sense for you. For example, Rabbi Silver decided to focus on creativity. But he had many choices along this path. He decided to continue with his religious orientation and make sculptures of biblical figures. He could have adventured into an entirely new subject area, or he might have kept searching for the medium that best suited him.

We all have the opportunity to decide if we want to continue what we were doing in some fashion, try something novel, search for a new path, relax and let life emerge, stay involved but as a spectator, or retreat to the couch. There is no "right" path. Each one presents benefits and challenges. You may set out on a path consciously or unconsciously, and you may start on one path even before retiring and, after a while, switch to another.

On the basis of research for my books on retirement, I have identified six major paths that retirees follow. These paths are general categories. The decisions you face about your next steps are ones you have faced at previous times and will face again. But these paths have something in common—they can serve as a framework for your new life, a context that can help you make more specific decisions about your future.

As you imagine what's next, let's begin by reviewing the paths I described in *Retire Smart, Retire Happy: Finding Your True Path in Life*. Then we will go a step further and consider the pros and cons of each. The question to ask yourself is, "Is this a path that will serve my need to matter to myself, to others, or the community at large?"[16]

Continuers

Continuers still identify with their previous work, home, or volunteer life. They continue to use existing skills, interests, and activities but modify them to fit retirement. Continuers have the advantage of maintaining their identity because they gradually, rather than abruptly, shift the way they see themselves and present themselves to the world. President Jimmy Carter continues to be a messenger for peace, writes books, and has invested energy in the Carter Center in Atlanta, Georgia—a reminder of who he was as president and what he is continuing to do for the world.

Another Continuer, William, a retired university dean and professor, decided to remain in the university town. He continued on his academic path, writing books and attending professional meetings. He stayed in touch with former colleagues who still worked at the university and contacted others around the world by e-mail. His latest book was considered the major textbook in his field. Jessie, another continuer who was once a seamstress in a dry cleaning establishment, continued making clothes for her children and grandchildren.

The positive side of being a Continuer is the comfort of having a predictable life—one based on the routines and interests that you already have found rewarding. On the other hand, if you are too concentrated on doing what you have always done, you may miss other, rewarding opportunities or options—ones that were not available to you during your work life.

Easy Gliders

Easy Gliders separate from the past and take each day as it comes. It is instructive to consider how Sam, also a former university dean and a book-writing colleague of William's went in such a different direction even though Sam and William had spent their working years writing together. Yet when Sam retired, he became an avid poker player, golfer, and connoisseur of the arts. After 2 years, he volunteered as a docent at an art museum. There he drove a tram, taking people from building to building on the museum grounds. He disengaged from his professional life, and like other Easy Gliders, he enjoyed having unscheduled time, no set agenda, and the ability to select activities that appealed to him as they presented themselves.

An Easy Glider may spend one day visiting a friend, the next one going to the beach or on a shopping spree, and the next visiting the library. They luxuriate in their newfound freedom—whatever feels right. The joy of having no agenda and no pressure makes for a relaxed life. But there is a downside. Easy Gliding is not necessarily a perpetual vacation. Once you've had a chance to drift for a while, the result of having so much unstructured time can lead to boredom, which can make you feel you no longer matter.

Adventurers

Adventurers move in new directions. They see retirement as an opportunity to make daring changes in their lives. They may have retired from one career, returned to school, and started another career. In *Retire Smart, Retire Happy*, I wrote about Bob, a researcher who—despite the skepticism of his friends—became a massage therapist.[17] A year after my book was published, Bob died of cancer. Later, his wife recalled,

> Some of those men who had scoffed at him when he made the decision to become a massage therapist later told him how much they admired him. Personally, I was thrilled reading the book, because it made me realize how courageous Bob had been to go to something entirely new.

Jane, a retired administrative assistant in the school system, turned her hobby of raising goats into her new life. She bought a small farm, where she is raising cashmere and angora goats. She also has llamas, alpacas, free-range chickens, and peacocks. The change has permeated her life. She never wears stockings or makeup; her day is organized around feeding and caring for the animals. She occasionally sees former friends from the education world, but her total immersion in the farm has taken over her life. She's also given up her car and only drives a truck.

Dee, a retired administrator from the U.S. State Department, was a participant in a focus group I ran. After retiring, she bought a Harley and took lessons in motorcycle riding—a dramatic change, to be sure. At this writing, she is getting certified as a motorcycle instructor and claims she is having the time of her life.

The benefits of Adventuring are clear: You can ferret out your regrets and follow your bliss, feeling energized and creative. However, if the adventure does not work out, you could be disappointed, facing once again the urgent question, Now what do I do? Jane knows she matters to the animals, and she feels productive in her farm venture. Although the rewards have been great, the personal and financial investment required might make it hard for her to continue in her adventure. If that happens, she can go back to the drawing board to figure out her next steps. This is reminiscent of the trial-and-error period that often follows graduation from high school or college. You keep trying one path after another until you find the right fit.

Searchers

Searchers have separated from the main activities of their past but have not yet found the "right" path. Often a Searcher has already tried being a Continuer, Adventurer, or Easy Glider but has felt the need to shift gears. Searchers try Plan A, B, C, D, and so on until they discover their path.

There are two kinds of Searchers. One is looking for a permanent niche, like the woman who served on one board after another, trying to find something that gave her a feeling of permanence. The other kind loves the process of exploration, with the potential of continuously pursuing different avenues and experiences. Bob went on a solo sailing trip, Ruth went to a retreat where she learned to meditate, and Cathy took a course on Kabbalah. The form of their searches differed, but the goal of their quest was the same: to reflect on what they had learned in their lives and how they wanted to spend their remaining years.

The path of the Searcher can be enticing because it offers the hope of rewarding opportunities and many options for happiness. This is especially true for the type of Searchers who love the search itself. However, the downside is that they can continue searching, never landing on something meaningful. If the search becomes troublesome with no resolution in sight, some sessions with a career counselor could help. Most community colleges have a career counseling center available to the public, usually charging a small fee for counseling.

Involved Spectators

Involved Spectators still care deeply about their previous work. They are no longer major players, but they compensate by finding ways to expose themselves to the people, ideas, and activities that made their work rewarding. Sam was a Washington lobbyist who for health reasons could no longer walk the halls of Congress. But he remained a news junkie, and he belonged to groups where political discussions kept him energized and connected. Sara, a retired museum curator, continued to study art and to visit museums as a spectator.

When one woman heard me speak about this path, she exclaimed, "Now I know what I want to put on my card—'Involved Spectator.'" This path offers the opportunity to stay alert and knowledgeable about your field. The danger is that this path might keep you too rooted in your past and might be a painful reminder that you no longer matter in the scene you loved. As one involved spectator reported, "I am about yesterday. I don't like the feeling, but it is my reality."

Retreaters

Retreaters find that the struggle to participate actively in anything beyond daily, required routines requires too much energy. Retreating is not necessarily a permanent state, and retreaters are not all the same. Some Retreaters have given up on finding ways to replace the purpose they'd had when working. Others may just need a moratorium to figure out how to approach their new life and all the changes that accompany retirement.

A participant in one of my retirement workshops told his parents' story. Harry and Bea retired together and moved to a different state. At first, Harry spent his days sitting around the house, not focusing on any particular interest or activity. Bea joined an amateur painting group in which each person was expected to submit works for a biannual art show. She had three paintings ready to enter but did not want to spend the money to frame them. She literally begged Harry to make her frames. He finally agreed and found he was good at it—even liked it. He later emerged from his retreat and became the official framer for the group.

Retreating for a while can be a positive way to clear your head and relax before searching for your next commitment. But some retreaters are deeply confused and upset after retirement. They miss their former coworkers and have not been able to make new friends. They find that losing their work constitutes a blow to their egos. They retreat to their couch to watch TV, and they withdraw from friends and family.

If you find yourself or someone close to you pursuing the retreater path, try to assess whether it's depression or just a time out. Betty Friedan, in her landmark book *The Fountain of Age*, suggested that depression can be a natural response to loss of power and purpose.[18]

Nathan Billig, a geriatric psychiatrist and author of *To Be Old and Sad: Understanding Depression in the Elderly*, agreed that many older people experience depression around a particular situation for understandable reasons, such as the loss of someone close or a diagnosis of a medical problem. The same could apply to a retired person who feels a loss of colleagues, structure, or purpose. But chronic depression is different. It is a set of symptoms that interfere with daily functioning.[19] You can benefit from professional help for depression that is tied to your situation; you need both medical and psychological intervention when depression is chronic. The good news is that today, with proper diagnosis, depression is treatable. If you think that it may be depression, this is the time to seek professional help.

PUT YOUR PASSION AND PATH TOGETHER

You can get some direction for your future by thinking about the two things we've just covered: your passion—learning, creating, working, volunteering, kinkeeping, or playing—and your path—being a Continuer, Adventurer, Searcher, Easy Glider, Involved Spectator, or Retreater. By putting these together, you will gain some direction for your future Purpose.

Sally, a librarian considering retirement, provides an example of how to put passion and path together. During her career, Sally spent much of her day indoors, at a desk, developing close relationships with the library patrons. Occasionally she joined friends for dinner, but her main focus was her pride in her job. At some point, she realized that she needed to start thinking about retirement, but the thought of being away from her work routine made her apprehensive. She couldn't imagine what she would do when she lost her daily connections and purpose.

A resourceful person, Sally sought help from a career counselor. During the counseling sessions, she spoke enthusiastically about her love of cooking, noting that she'd enjoyed making brownies and other goodies for library events such as children's hours and staff meetings. As a result of the counseling, she decided to explore ways to turn her interest into a retirement career. After taking a class with a pastry chef and spending a month-long vacation in Italy studying with a famous chef, Sally came up with a plan: She would become a caterer. She identified a catering business that might employ her. Now that she had a plan, her apprehensiveness turned into excitement. Her efforts will no doubt facilitate a happy retirement.

Exhibit 5.1 shows how Sally's chart looked as she embarked on her retirement career. Striking out into a totally different field clearly qualified her as an Adventurer. Referring to herself as "Chef Sally" provided a new creative and working focus. The decision to become a caterer gave her a new purpose—a theme that could give her meaning and happiness as well as a feeling of accomplishment.

EXHIBIT 5.1. Sally's Retirement Passion and Path

Passion and focus	Continuer	Adventurer	Searcher	Easy Glider	Involved Spectator	Retreater	Other
					Path		
Creativity		Opened her mind to new endeavors with a creative flair.					
Learning		Studied to become a chef and a caterer.					
Working	Planned to become a chef and a caterer.						
Volunteering							
Kinkeeping							
Playing							

Conclusion

Because we are living longer and our circumstances will change, our path, too, will change, and possibly our passion. It's important to realize that you may want or need to change your direction and your goals several times during your retirement. A new retiree said to me, "I have always had a mission statement about what I am doing. I am now without that. But I will use the next year to create my new mission." Her attitude is positive and will result in what's needed: a new "mission possible." You have the tools; just remember that finding your new mission takes time, energy, and commitment.

It's Your Turn: Tips on How to Reshape Your Purpose

1. Identify Your Passion or Focus

Think about where you want to spend your energy. Would you like to spend your time

- creating new projects?
- learning new things?
- working in a new line of work, cutting back to part time, or becoming an entrepreneur?
- volunteering?
- kinkeeping?
- playing?
- something else?

2. Plan Specific Ways to Enhance Your Focus

If you have chosen to create new projects, brainstorm some ideas about what they might be. If you want to learn new things, hone in on learning possibilities.

3. Consider the Pros and Cons of the Paths You Are Considering

Choose the path or paths that make sense for you, and list the pros and cons of each:

- Continuer
- Adventurer
- Searcher
- Easy Glider
- Involved Spectator
- Retreater

4. Rehearse Your Future Passion or Path

It can be helpful to anticipate your future and actually rehearse how the scenario might evolve. Take the example of geographical relocation: If you have fantasized about moving to another city and state, try it out first. You might take a 2-week vacation in the middle of winter, you might spend 2 weeks during another season, or you might take a 2-month leave of absence and get to know the place. After this rehearsal, you will know if this move is what you want.

For example, if you are considering a move to New Mexico, visit 1 month a year for several years before you move. Ask, "Is this what I really want or where I want to be?"

III

CREATING YOUR OWN HAPPINESS

6

It's About You: Design Your Own Psychological Portfolio

This book has been about successful strategies people have used to build their Psychological Portfolios. It is now time to turn your attention to your own. The next three chapters cover angles for you to consider as you figure out how to strengthen your portfolio in retirement. Your first consideration should be to focus on possible stumbling blocks as you proceed.

OVERCOME ROADBLOCKS WHEN LIFE GETS IN THE WAY

Clearly, there are detours that could become obstacles as you move ahead. Whatever the roadblock, it is important, if possible, to identify it beforehand. Two frequently encountered roadblocks are the difficulties of planning and the prevalence of stereotyping.

The Planning Conundrum

Even though none of us can predict the future, we know that planning, though unsettling, is a necessary guide to our future. But many do not plan. Why?

In his book *Stumbling on Happiness*, Daniel Gilbert, Harvard University professor of psychology, explained that "planning requires that we peer into our futures, and anxiety is one of the reactions we may have when we do"[1] because it is impossible to imagine every aspect of the future. This might explain why some retirees migrate to warmer climates but then return to their original homes. They had not thought out all the scenarios. They might not have considered the high cost of living in the new community, the extent to which they would miss long-time friends and family, or changes in their health and financial resources.

I decided to explore this issue with some younger baby boomers. I asked them to tell me how they envisioned their future. They seemed stumped. So invested in their current, complicated lives, balancing work and family demands, their future seemed far away. They saw problems rather than possibilities. Their number one issue related to whether or not they would outlive their money, and number two, they were scared about the possibility of needing to provide caregiving for others because they had observed many family and friends already in that role.

Despite the anxiety that planning raised, Gilbert found that people routinely think about the future.[2] Doris and Jim are examples of people who think about their futures, free of anxiety. Doris was the omelet cook at a restaurant I visit frequently. She complained that her arm got tired and ached at night. She was looking forward to retirement; the physical strain connected with her job was taking a toll. In fact, she started planning ahead by enrolling in a training program at the local children's hospital so that she could start volunteering as soon as she stopped working.

My first interview with Jim was several months before he was to retire from a government agency. I asked what excited him as he considered retirement. He answered that he had been thinking a great deal about it and saw it as a time to

> reinvent myself, have time to lecture and write, mentor students in public relations, learn how to cook/speak Spanish/dance the tango, spend several weeks in a foreign city, read fiction, learn more about how to relax and be patient.

When I asked what scared him about retirement, his list included "finding comprehensive medical insurance to cover me from 60 to 65, establishing a new routine and identity outside of work, staying healthy and maintaining a regular exercise schedule." Jim had thought ahead about ways to keep in touch with his work colleagues, and he hoped to work 2 days a week as a consultant at his old agency for at least the first year of his retirement. In my follow-up interview several months after he retired, he expressed some ambivalence. Life was not perfect; however, he was committed to make it rewarding.

Like Doris and Jim, many are able to plan ahead and even enjoy the process. But for those who don't or can't plan for retirement, it could be for one of the following reasons:

- Their energy is in the present and not the future.
- They deny that retirement involves major transitions.
- They feel unable to forecast the future with any degree of accuracy.

Stereotyping

How many times have you heard people say, "I will not get that job or invitation because I am a woman [an older person, a person of color, a retiree]." It is difficult to untangle whether your reaction is based on the real world or whether you are setting up internal roadblocks. The AARP initiated an experiment in which two individuals with the same credentials, one 57 years old and the other 32 years old, applied for the same entry-level jobs. The younger person received a more favorable response about 60% of the time. Sally Dunaway, an AARP lawyer, reported that bias is beginning "at younger and younger ages. It used to be 65. Now it is 55, 48, or even 42."[3] But consider the conflicting message—men and women in their 70s are being elected to public office. Age is both relevant and irrelevant.

The late sociologist Bernice Neugarten framed the topic of bias in terms of one's *social clock*.[4] She explained that during childhood, our lives are determined by our biological clocks. In the adult years, our social clocks determine our behavior. For example, we ask, "Am I too young to retire? Is retirement at the right time for me?" We appraise our family life and ask, "Am I 'on' or 'off' time? Are my children 'on' or 'off' time"?

Our social clocks reflect the norms of our culture, social class, gender, age, and ethnic identification. Different cultures have different expectations about when to marry, have children, retire, move away from parents, pay your own health insurance, and so forth. These social clocks determine the way we stereotype others and ourselves. They can become formidable roadblocks if we say, "I am too old at 72 to pursue a new career" or "I am not old enough at 45 to retire." Birthday cards promote negatives about aging. Comments like, "It is all downhill after 40" or "I am having a senior moment" or "She is losing it" reflect our expectation that our bodies and brains are diminishing as we age.

Recently, Michelle reported, "I am a has-been." She had been turned down for a big consulting job for which she thought she was a shoo-in. The reason given was the economy; however, she attributed it to her age. When Lon, a construction worker, found out that a much younger woman was selected for the job he was applying for, he attributed it to his age. We will never know the truth. We can only hope that Michelle and Lon will not let age stand in the way of their efforts to achieve their goals.

Perhaps there is little we, as individuals, can do about the world's youth obsession. But we can challenge our own stereotypes about retiring and aging. The evidence is clear: No matter what our age, there is time to grow and explore the unknown and also to change course.

ESTABLISH A NEW STRUCTURE

Retirement is probably the first time since kindergarten that you've lived without a daily structure. After Carlos retired from a government agency, he became a real estate broker. Three years ago, he quit all work. He shared the following insight with me:

> My entire life has focused on the future. In school, my parents expected good grades so I could get into college; in college, I was expected to get prepared for the future so I could support myself and a family; while working, I had to manage my finances so our future would be secure. This is the first time that my life has not been geared toward the future. I am in the here and now, and it is such a good feeling.

For some people, like Carlos, living without a structure is not a problem; for others, it is very difficult. One person from the retired volunteer focus group described in the Introduction of this volume defined *structure* as an individual's plan for the day, the week, the month, or even the year. Many felt that having structure in their lives helped answer questions such as the following: What do you do when you wake up? Do you dress for the day, hang around in night clothes, dress for exercising? Do you keep a calendar and check it? Some of the retirees plan each day in detail, and others prefer letting the day unfold spontaneously. Some need the structure of a calendar with activities listed for each day; others prefer empty pages. The trick is to figure out how much structure versus free-floating time you need to have a happy life. Your personality will play a part in these decisions.

Some retirees, excited at first by the idea of unlimited free time, discover that too little on their schedule can lead to boredom. So they turn to the task of building a structure to replace the one they had when they were working. Joining health clubs, establishing workout schedules, meeting for walks, signing up for classes, and visiting grandchildren on a regular basis are some ways people build a schedule. One man told me his structure was dictated by visiting doctors, accountants, and stockbrokers.

Let's consider how a newly retired single woman built structure into her life. Dot retired from her full-time job, immediately set up a home office, and designed business cards identifying herself as a consultant. She found that the only way to make the transition from her previous whirlwind days to days with practically no interaction with others was to intentionally build a daily and weekly structure. She went to the gym 3 days a week, made lunch dates several times a week, and made sure that she had at least two activities each day. After 3 years, she went back to work full time. She has found it difficult to get the balance right.

Back to Jim, who had given so much thought to planning for retirement: After 4 months, he reported,

> The good news, now that I am alternating 5 days off and 2 days at work, is that each day can feel like a blank slate. The bad news: Each day can feel like a blank slate! Indeed, during the first month of this new routine, I felt disoriented—occasionally waking up wondering what day it was!

After the "exhilaration of the first 2 months," he finally began figuring out a schedule that would implement his earlier goals. He set aside Mondays, Wednesdays, and Fridays to spend 2 hours at a nearby hotel fitness center. In addition, he enrolled in two courses, one in art and the other in architecture. On Tuesdays and Thursdays, he did consulting work for his former employer. He concluded, "The obvious lesson is the more free time I have, the more I have to plan my time." He started keeping a diary as a way to figure out the right balance for himself.

CHART YOUR PORTFOLIO

I revisit Rabbi Silver as a model for your own path. In chapter 5, I told the story of his retirement transition. He represented the sixth generation of rabbis in his family and had had a clear sense of Purpose throughout his career—a life committed to Judaism, to scholarly pursuits, to involvement with his congregation around issues of theology and coping with life, and to living a meaningful life. During his career, his Psychological

Portfolio was strong. The strategies he used to maintain this strength after he retired are instructive.

Rabbi Silver followed a combination path of Continuer and Adventurer (for descriptions of these paths, see chap. 5 of this volume, "Choose Your Retirement Path" section). When he retired, his congregation built him a "retirement study," an office that served as a base to keep him connected to his religious activities. As an elder statesman to his successors and their aides, he continued to counsel congregants who sought his advice and even wrote a book about his retirement transition. In his life as a Continuer, the rabbi maintained his Identity as a religious leader, maintained Relationships with the congregation and staff of the synagogue, and had a continuing commitment to the religious Purposes he assumed when he became a rabbi.

But he was also an Adventurer. Discovering his talent and enthusiasm for sculpting resulted in a strong psychological portfolio. The serious commitment to sculpture shaped a whole new Identity for him; he developed new Relationships with mentors and other artists, and he found a Purpose that unleashed his creative energies and added contentment to his retirement life.

Although in my analysis I have continually treated the three parts of the Psychological Portfolio separately, we can see from Rabbi Silver's chart (see Exhibit 6.1) that they really are interrelated. If you strengthen one, in most cases the others will also be strengthened. Rabbi Silver's scaled-back career and hobby of sculpting took him down two different paths. He was a Continuer

EXHIBIT 6.1. Rabbi Silver's Path and Portfolio Guide

Portfolio component		Path					
	Continuer	Adventurer	Searcher	Easy Glider	Involved Spectator	Retreater	Other
Identity	Counselor Scholar Mentor	Sculptor Artist					
Relationships	Colleagues Congregation	Other artists					
Purpose and focus	Religious practice	Creator					

because of his teaching and studying and an Adventurer because of his sculpting. These two paths jump-started his retirement. With a relatively unfettered chunk of time and a financial base, he created a new lifestyle with the potential for being as rewarding as the career he had followed before retiring.

By devoting time and energy to analyzing your own retirement options, you too can design a rewarding future. Record your answers in Exhibit 6.2. This will give you a snapshot of how your portfolio will look based on the path(s) you choose. Estimate where the strengths of your Identity, Relationships, and Purpose fall on the chart depending on each path you are considering. For example, if you are on a Continuer path, fill out the chart based on that analysis. If you want to be an Adventurer, then fill in the chart to reflect the impact on your Identity, Relationships, and Purpose. This chart can help you decide what your next steps should be. For example, think of two alternative paths you might pursue. Then fill out Exhibit 6.2 for each path, asking yourself which path will enhance your Identity, Relationships, and Purpose.

CONCLUSION

Charting your course is comparatively easy when using the graphs and projecting the roadblocks that could detour your progress. Sometimes we are our own worst enemies when we imagine that we are not qualified or too old or decrepit to take on a new dream. We have the

EXHIBIT 6.2. Your Path and Portfolio Guide

Portfolio component	Path					
	Continuer	Adventurer	Searcher	Easy Glider	Involved Spectator	Retreater	Other
Identity							
Relationships							
Purpose and focus							

power to stop our negative thinking and to face the future with energy as we build new structure into our lives. Remember Rabbi Silver's words: "Retirement is a gift—an opportunity not to be squandered."

It's Your Turn: Tips on How to Make Your Portfolio Work

1. Read About the Future

Do you find it difficult to plan ahead? If so, I recommend reading Daniel Gilbert's *Stumbling on Happiness*.[5] As you read, make notes about new ways to think about your future. Overcome your fears of retirement planning.

2. Use a Surrogate

Interview retirees to find out what the future might be like. For example, if you think you might like to become a mediator, shadow someone who is doing that. Find out whether you would respond well to the training and the types of cases you might be assigned. Then decide whether it is the path for you.

3. Think About Your Body and Soul

How will you deal with your own health if it becomes compromised? You will be forced to care for your body as it ages. Will you attend to your spiritual life as you confront aging and retirement issues for yourself and your family?

4. Fight Stereotyping

Come to terms with your own aging. How do you feel when someone you don't know refers to you as "old" or "too old"? Do you feel that experience and wisdom are enhancing your life as you get older? Or are you more concerned about getting rid of your wrinkles and appearing younger? How will you "face your face" and deal with your own age bias as well as possible discrimination?

If you are stuck, help figure out where the "stuckness" comes from. It can result from either internal attitudes (e.g., "I am too old to try that out"; "I am not flexible enough"; "I don't know what I really want to do") or external factors (e.g., "There are no part-time jobs for older people in my field"). Figuring out where the problem lies is the basis for designing a course of action.

5. Identify Roadblocks

Identify the roadblocks that interfere with your moving ahead. Then brainstorm ways to overcome them. You might seek professional help, talk with friends, read a book, or join a support group. But whatever you decide, do something.

Your major roadblocks:

1._____
2._____

Your plan to overcome them:

1._____

2._____

3._____

6. Establish a Structure—Keep a Time Diary

A time diary helps you see how you structure your time and provides a baseline so that you can plan ahead. Let's say your plan was to reconnect with people you cared about in the past, but you have not made any progress. If you write down all of your activities during, say, a week in your life, you will clearly see if there is a disconnect between what you say you want to do and how you actually spend your time. You can then either modify your time or change your goals.

7. Strengthen Your Psychological Portfolio

Will the choices you make for retirement enable you to pursue your passion and purpose? Consider two avenues as you evaluate your current situation and project into the future: (a) where to focus your energy— your purpose and passion—and (b) strategies you will use to reach future goals. As you anticipate the challenges ahead, consider the following questions: Have you developed a narrative about your future self and life? Have you thought about your Identity after retirement?

8. Take a Retirement Seminar or Course

Think of retirement as an evolution of your career. Look at your interests, values, abilities, and opportunities as a way to plan next steps. If you choose to sign up for a seminar, make sure that it covers the psychological aspects connected with retirement. Although most of the advertised seminars focus on finances, many courses, lectures, and workshops are now covering both.

9. Be Open to Invitations

The power of invitation is compelling; try to be open to it. My involvement with the community organization SCOPE, described in chapter 1 of this volume,[6] resulted from receiving an invitation to participate in the organization's aging project. At first I said I was too busy. The person who invited me persisted. I finally said yes, and I am so glad I did!

10. Meet With a Counselor, Therapist, or Career Coach

For some people, taking a course, reading a book, or joining a group such as the Women's Retirement Group I discussed in chapter 4 of this volume may not be enough. You can locate a professionally trained helper to assist you in charting a new plan of action by contacting the American Counseling Association, the

American Psychological Association, or the National Association of Social Workers.

Your retirement challenge is to choose a life that makes you feel as if you count. That requires planning ahead and making a commitment to devote the energy to make the necessary changes.

7

Three Guidelines for a Better Retirement

Martha, an insurance agent in her 60s, announced her early retirement because she did not want to be seen as hanging on too long. She did not think she would ace her coming retirement; in fact, she was "terrified" of the future. She could not imagine what she would do. During our interview, she asked if there were a road map to follow as she transitioned from work to something new. She was retiring from a full-time career where she had a strong professional Identity, meaningful colleague Relationships, and a clear sense of Purpose. Giving up what you have before knowing what's next can be scary. To deal with major changes like Martha's, I suggest three guidelines: take a transition perspective, apply the wisdom factor, and prepare for surprises.

GUIDELINE 1: TAKE A TRANSITION PERSPECTIVE

Martha, and every other person who makes a major change, is in transition. In fact, transitions are what happen to us all through life. We always seem to be leaving one way of life and moving on to another. However, just telling Martha, "You'll be okay, you're in transition" does not help her understand why transitions can be challenging and perplexing. Ruth Lee Silver, Rabbi Silver's wife, described her retirement as a bundle of many transitions that took time to incorporate. The operative word is *time:* time to mourn for what you left, time to figure out what's next, and time to feel comfortable with a new life. Ruth Lee explained the process as she experienced it:

> When my husband told me that he was thinking about retirement, I was paralyzed with fear. The weekend my husband retired was filled with 3 days of adulation from the entire community. Rather than basking in all his praise, I cried until my mascara dripped onto my clothing and my children worried that I was having a teeny-weeny nervous breakdown.
>
> I was crying at the idea of retirement. I wondered what I would do all day. I had worked on a newspaper—not exactly the *New York Times*, but it was intoxicating. For the last 14 years I thought I was a combination of Maureen Dowd and everybody who wrote for the style sections of the *Times*, but now I found myself more in God's waiting room than in paradise. As for me, an abject failure in what a friend called "retirement skills," a dropout from bridge, canasta, mah-jongg, and golf, I wondered what I would do all day.
>
> Fast forward 13 years. I didn't die down here in Florida. I sit on the terrace and watch the pelicans and I enjoy watching my husband enjoying [life]. I have started painting and my work is regularly shown in art shows. I still write occasional articles for the paper.

The odds are that you will be disappointed if you expect a wonderful new life on your first day of retirement. We can learn from Ruth Lee and many others who, after a long struggle, feel satisfied with their lives. The lesson is that transitions take time. If you allow yourself time to grieve over the things that you will miss from your previous life and give yourself time to recognize that things will come together as you start working on "getting a life," you will have a good shot at happiness.

Ruth Lee made many new friends and found a community of like-minded people. She developed a new outlet for her creative endeavors as an artist—and her identity remained intact. Her case illustrates that it is possible to deal with all of the expected and unexpected transitions that can continually occur through our lives.

A Theory to Explain Your Transitions

You can understand your transitions if you look at the three major parts of transition theory:

1. Examine the degree to which your life has been altered through changes in your roles, relationships, routines, and assumptions.
2. Locate where you are in the transition process (considering a change, beginning the change, 2 years after the change).
3. Identify the resources you can apply to making it a success.

Transitions are both events—like having a baby, retiring, or becoming a mother-in-law—and non-events—like not having the baby you expected, the job promotion you felt entitled to, or the retirement you had planned. Whether the transition is positive, negative, or neutral, the critical issue is the degree to which it alters your roles, relationships, routines, and assumptions.

Ruth Lee began to think she might be in "God's waiting room," reflecting a different set of assumptions than she had when she was writing for a newspaper. Her husband's retirement shifted her professional role, changed her relationships and daily routines, and altered the way she saw herself. The more your life changes, the more stress you experience. It is for that reason that many experts recommend a phased retirement so that you can adjust to these changes gradually.

Some transitions, like changing apartments in the same city, will change your routines—where you pick up your coffee in the morning or drop off your dry cleaning—but your roles and relationships are not necessarily altered. However, moving to a new city and starting a new job change more aspects of your life, requiring that you mobilize more resources for coping.

An example of a transition that changes everything is losing a parent, especially when the last parent dies. This transition changes your role as adult child; severs your relationship from the preceding generation; changes your routine of daily, weekly, or monthly calls to your parent; and changes your assumption that life goes on forever. Your anchor is gone. One woman described the devastation she experienced when she removed her father's name from her address book. She said,

> It is the single most devastating unspoken tragedy of my adult life. There is also a sideways slam, a crushing sign of your own mortality. I guess all I can do is just remember to get a hug from someone close a few extra times until it gets easier to cope.

Transition events and nonevents do not happen in a moment; they are a gradual process. Again, *time* is the operative word: Transitions take time, and people's reactions to them change—for better or worse—while they are underway. At first, people think of nothing but being a new graduate, a new widow, a recent retiree. Then, like Ruth Lee, they begin to separate from the past and move toward the new role, for a while teetering between the two. I interviewed a man who had retired 6 months previously from the public school system. His first month was very difficult, because he was accustomed to his routine, his relationships, and his professional identity. A year later, he was comfortable with his new life. He was in an exercise program, served as a volunteer for the court system as a guardian ad litem, and was becoming active with the League of Women Voters.

Each person approaches getting a new life in a unique way, with a different set of resources. I call them the four Ss—situation, self, supports, and strategies:[1]

- **■** *situation:* Your situation at the time of transition affects your options for the future. Are there other stresses? For example, if one's significant other becomes critically ill, coping with retirement becomes more difficult. One woman reported that within a year of retiring, her husband had a major stroke. Her situation became one of intensive care-giving for a very ill loved one.

- *self*: Clearly, your personal characteristics influence how you will cope with your situation. Are you optimistic, resilient, and able to deal with ambiguity?

- *supports*: The supports you receive or that are available at the time of your transition are critical to your sense of well-being. For example, if a recent retiree moves to a new city knowing no one and with no supports, his or her adaptation might be slowed down.

- *strategies*: There is no magic coping strategy. If you use lots of strategies flexibly, you will be better able to cope. Most coping strategies can be categorized into one of the following: those aimed at changing the problem (problem solving, assertiveness, lawsuits), those that change the meaning of the problem (trying to see the glass as half full), and those that help manage stress (meditation, yoga, swimming).[2]

If Martha had asked whether this was the best time to retire, I would have suggested that she examine her four Ss and ask herself, "Is my situation good at this time? Do I bring a resilient self to the move? Do I have enough supports? Do I have lots of coping strategies in my repertoire?" If all Martha's Ss are positive, a retirement move might be a good decision. However, if her situation is problematic or her supports are minimal, she might make a decision to delay. And, of course, finances must be factored into the equation.

We have seen that planning ahead can sometimes be problematic, and negotiating transitions can be tricky. However, knowledge about the transition process can alleviate the confusing feelings that often go along with transitions.

GUIDELINE 2: APPLY THE WISDOM FACTOR

Lillian B. Rubin, sociologist and author, wrote that as we live longer, healthier lives, we face "uncharted territory":

> After organizing our lives around the pursuit of a goal—raising the children, writing a book, getting tenure, a big promotion, winning the gold . . . we find that it's not the destination that has given life its meaning and continuity but the journey itself. I took myself out of the fast lane nearly three years ago and have no wish to go back. But that doesn't mean I don't still miss it.[3]

Her words reflect wisdom about life and retirement. Wisdom—something we often recognize when we see it but find hard to define—is critical as you make decisions. Wisdom is often associated with old age, but I suggest that wisdom knows no age. And in addition to a growing body of philosophical, empirical, and psychological approaches to the fuzzy, paradoxical study of wisdom, sociologist Monika Ardelt defined it in measurable ways and developed a Wisdom Scale. The scale consists of three separate but interconnected ways of dealing with the world:

1. *cognitive*—the ability to look at your situation and understand it;
2. *reflective*—the ability to step back and put what is happening into perspective; and
3. *emotional*—the ability to stay positive even when facing negative events and to accept conflicting emotions.[4]

As Martha considered her retirement, I suggested that she ask herself if she had the information she needed about the challenges ahead (cognitive), the power to reflect on the information she would gather (reflective), and the ability to deal with the emotional ups and downs that follow any transition (emotional). I think Martha, or anyone for that matter, can apply these three components of wisdom as they consider what's next. The next sections discuss each component in turn.

The Cognitive Ingredient

The cognitive ingredient addresses what you need to know to make wise decisions. Selecting the "right" path depends on *informed intuition:* that combination of good information with a "gut" feeling that this is the right thing for you to do. Malcolm Gladwell, author of *Blink: The Power of Thinking Without Thinking* and staff writer for the *New Yorker* magazine, studied intuitive decisions. What looks like a snap judgment might be what he labeled *thin-slicing,* or the "ability of our unconscious to find patterns in situations and behavior based on very narrow slices of experience."[5] On the basis of your own thin-slicing, you can begin to figure out what course to follow. In each case, your ability to cope with decisions can be enhanced by searching for the information and options that can help you resolve them.

Let's return to the financial analogy I used in the Introduction of this volume. To avoid financial problems, you arm yourself with knowledge. Being aware of the dollars-and-cents challenges and figuring out how to meet these challenges helps control fear about the unknown that can occur with the loss of a regular paycheck or a changing economy. The same is true for your psychological concerns.

You know that many people experience jolts in their Identity, changes in their work and personal Relationships, and an eroding loss of Purpose. As one man said, "I don't know what to do after I read the paper and walk the dog." Another man, recently widowed, squandered an enormous amount of money traveling, buying new things, and moving to an upscale apartment as a way to compensate for his loneliness. He assumed that he would always feel frantic. Later, he realized,

> If only someone had told me that over time I would come to terms with my loss, I might not have sold my house and moved so quickly. The pain would have remained, but knowledge that there is an end in sight would have acted as a control on my behavior.

Information about the transition process would not have eliminated his discomfort, but it could have provided the knowledge he needed to calm down and delay rash decision making. He was thin-slicing too much.

The more you acknowledge issues like the ones discussed here, and the more you think about how you can or would address them in your own life, the better your chances for having a happy retirement.

The Reflective Ingredient

Retirement provides time to reflect on your life—where you have been, where you are now, and where you are going. Musing about your past and speculating about your future will put your life in perspective as you make decisions about what to do next.

We reflect and evaluate our success by comparing where we are in life with our notion of what we believe is appropriate for our circumstances. Second, we reflect on time—time left to live; time left to complete some tasks; time left to pursue old dreams; and time left to make a success, or more of a success, of life. I was puzzled when my aunt, bedridden and dying, redid her house. As I look back, I realize she had been unwilling to say, "This is the end." She needed, as we all do, to have a goal, to still believe there is time left to accomplish some tasks.

There is much in the literature about reflecting on your past, which gerontologists label *life review*. At the same time, it is important to keep your focus future oriented. A retired football star can choose to review his past fame and his great plays, or he can put them in perspective and start thinking about coaching kids. We need to combine acknowledging our past with seeing how it can fit into a meaningful future.

We reflect on our lives each time we weather or initiate a major transition. In her book *60 on Up: The Truth About Aging in America*, Rubin provided an honest appraisal of the losses and gains that accompanied her retirement.[6] Instead of remaining in an academic life, she became engaged in art and had the thrill of selling a painting.

Retirement is an opportunity to face regrets and to begin to consider ways to come to terms with them. In college, Daniel had dreamed of writing Broadway musicals. However, he married and quickly had two children. Instead of pursuing a career in music, he followed in his father's footsteps and became a lawyer. Through the years, Daniel regretted his decision. He saw his retirement as an opportunity to return to music, and he volunteered at a senior center where he played the piano in the lobby. He provided an uplifting welcome to those who entered the center.

With every transition, you are giving up part of your life while simultaneously engaging in new ventures. This exchange theory is a helpful way to reflect on your life and on what you are getting in exchange for what you are giving up. I interviewed Don for the PBS special, *Retire Smart, Retire Happy*[7] and asked how he felt when his calls to former colleagues were not returned immediately. He told me he expected less responsiveness from his former coworkers. He had realized in advance that he would be giving up the recognition associated with his work in exchange for freedom to travel and study.

The Emotional Ingredient

Like any other major transition, retirement will inevitably produce mixed emotions. There will be ups and downs, whether you are a young retiring ballet dancer or an older retiring plumber. After all, you are leaving a familiar lifestyle and moving into uncharted territory. Part of wisdom is learning to manage your emotions when you are faced with challenges, especially transition challenges. I am reminded of some retirees who make decisions on the basis of the emotion of the moment. One couple moved a week after their retirement to a totally new community. Within 2 years, they were back "home." They felt as if they were on an emotional roller coaster.

Richard Lazarus, professor emeritus of psychology at the University of California, pioneered research on stress and emotion theory, which has particular relevance for retirement:

> What happens, especially with a strong emotion, is that we who are experiencing it are often taken over by the emotion: Our attention becomes riveted on the harm or benefit. . . . We are caught up in the charged relationship . . . with the environment."[8]

With his colleague, Susan Folkman, he developed a way for people to understand and control their emotional responses. If you feel negative about something, like moving to a new community, you have two choices: You can take action to change the part of the environment that is aggravating you. If that does not work, you can change your thinking about the situation.[9]

For example, if retirement is not going according to your plan, you can use problem-solving strategies, like brainstorming or negotiating, to take control and thereby make alternative plans. You try to figure out what you can do and how you can take action. If, on the other hand, you are in a situation that looks as if it cannot be changed, you can use emotion-focused strategies like reframing that enable you to view your situation in another way.

Several years ago, I had the opportunity to interview men and women employed by the U.S. Postal Service. I met Linda, a retired mail carrier, who explained how much she missed the interactions with people on her route. Over the years, she had established relationships with many of them. What a shock to go from being totally involved in work one day and the next day having nothing to do. She busied herself with housework, but she could not avoid her growing feeling of uselessness and depression. Then she read an article that urged readers to reframe their situation as a way to reduce their stress. She applied the advice to herself. She decided to see this period as a "cooling-down" period before making plans for her future. Thus, she used emotion-focused coping to get over the initial shock, and later she moved into the problem-focused phase to brainstorm next steps.

New research bolsters the importance of emotion-focused coping. Studies of students after the events of September 11, 2001, showed that those who could see beyond the immediate situation and try to incorporate positive emotions, like gratitude and hope, coped more effectively than those who became overwhelmed and negative. Apply this to retirement: If you are "failing" retirement, feel depressed, and are unable to gain a sense of control over yourself and your situation, you need to try to look for some positive thread and to see beyond the immediate situation. Researchers refer to this as the *broaden-and-build* theory of positive emotions: "The broadening triggered by positive emotions builds a range of resources" that will build resilience and result in positive outcomes.[10]

Retirement poses some practical issues. What can I, or we, afford to do financially? Is our house still the place where we really want to live, or should we look for one that's smaller or closer to the grandchildren? How do I want to fill the time that's available now that I'm not going to work every day? If there is any undisputable truth about retirement, it is that there are many paths to take and many ways to live your life. The options are endless, and you are not married to any one of them. But as you evaluate your situation and make decisions, remember to let wisdom, based on knowledge, reflection, and emotional control, trump knee-jerk reactions.

Guideline 3: Prepare for Surprises

Rather than *development, passages,* or *stages,* my pick for the best word to describe the adult years is *surprises.* Anthropologist Mary Catherine Bateson observed in her book *Composing a Life* that the adult years are not linear but fluid and even disjointed. She wrote,

> The model of an ordinary successful life that is held up for young people is one of early decision and commitment, often to an educational preparation that launches a single rising trajectory. . . . Many of society's casualties are men and women who assumed they had chosen a path in life and found that it disappeared in the underbrush.[11]

Bateson called adult life "an improvisatory art, about the ways we combine familiar and unfamiliar components in response to new situations." Her conclusions were based on her unusual upbringing (her parents were leading intellectuals Gregory Bateson and Margaret Mead) and her friendships with a number of women. She concluded that women's lives were characterized by discontinuity and, because of that, found life full of surprises.

The experience of my friend Ruth Caplin illustrates well that adult development and aging are about surprises—not about stages, ages, or passages. Thirty years ago, Ruth read a novel that entranced her. She bought a book about how to turn a novel into a screenplay. She wrote the screenplay, but when the novelist's family refused to grant permission to produce it, Ruth put the screenplay in a drawer and abandoned the project. Unknown to her, her son kept contacting the family and finally secured agreement to give Ruth the film rights. The movie—*Mrs. Palfrey at the Claremont*—was made, with Dame Joan Plowright as leading lady.[12] At 85, Ruth became what a friend of mine, Richard Levin, called an "LLC"—late-life celebrity.

Unfortunately, not all surprises are positive. You may be happily leading your life when suddenly you encounter age discrimination on your job, you receive a diagnosis of a life-threatening illness, or someone close to you dies. There are many ways in which we can be blindsided. A former student of mine finally returned to college to complete her bachelor's degree. In the middle of her program, her husband became critically ill, and she became his caregiver. They had part-time help, but the majority of the care was in her hands. Her life was put on hold; she was troubled about how to plan because of the ambiguity inherent in her situation. She withdrew from school.

Yes, retirement dreams can be derailed when events do not occur as expected. For example, Harry looked forward to enjoying retirement with his wife, Kim. They located a place to live in retirement and began planning in detail for their future. When Kim's mother became ill, requiring nursing care, their financial reserves were depleted. This unexpected situation required a dramatic change in plans. Instead of retiring and moving to North Carolina, they continued working. Kim's mother lived 7 more years. By the time she died, their dream of retiring and moving had moved out of reach.

Like Kim and Harry, as well as all those who are left with unrealized dreams, none of us can predict the specific surprises in store. But you should assume that you might have to go to Plan B when life does not follow your script. For example, Sarah was beginning to think about retirement. She had two plans—one if her husband lived a long time, and the other if she became a widow. She knew she needed to prepare for both. She rehearsed for surprises so that she could deal more effectively with the ambiguity and uncertainty that accompany any major transition.

CONCLUSION

Guidelines are only indicators, not gospel. To guide you, I have shared research on transitions and suggested that you apply the ingredients of wisdom—knowledge, reflection, and emotional control—to yourself. I also shared what I think is the bottom line about adult development and aging—that life is not a series of stages or even phases. Rather, it is filled with surprises—good and bad, expected and unexpected. And most important, you cannot assume that if you know someone is retired, you know anything about the person. Each person has a unique story that is unlike anyone else's.

IT'S YOUR TURN: YOUR TRANSITION TIPS

1. Consider Your Transition

Expressing thoughts aloud helps them become clear in your mind. So if you are retired, explain to someone else what you have learned about coping with this major transition. If you are thinking about retirement, share with someone else your thoughts about how you will cope with this major transition. Identify a friend, counselor, or support group to help you with this and future challenges.

2. Make Informed Decisions

You can benefit from others' experiences by interviewing one or two retirees you admire to see how they handled their challenges. Ask them to describe the emotions they experienced along the way and to reflect on their whole experience. And don't forget to ask for their advice.

3. Create a Plan B

Because you never know what is in store, plan ahead by writing two or three scenarios for your future. Update these as time goes on.

4. Identify Your Resources for Coping With Retirement

To help you know if you are ready for the future, identify your resources using the questions in Exhibit 7.1. Check the answer that reflects where you are strong. Then think about ways to strengthen the resources that need help.

EXHIBIT 7.1. Identify Your Resources for Coping in
Retirement: Sample Questions From the Transition Guide (TG)

The TG will enable you to take stock of your resources for
coping with change. Your resources include your situation, self,
supports, and strategies. Answering the following sample questions from the TG will give you an idea of which resources are
strong and which need strengthening.

Circle the number that best describes how each of your
resources is a help to you in retirement. If you have marked a
resource as a 4 or 5, it is a strong resource for you; if you
marked it as 1 or 2, you need to figure out ways to strengthen
it; if you marked it as 3, it is an in-between resource.

Your situation: How you see the transition						
1. Looking ahead, I feel able to . . .						
Plan ahead with great difficulty	1	2	3	4	5	Plan ahead with great ease
2. I see my situation as . . .						
Totally out of personal control	1	2	3	4	5	Totally within personal control
Your self: Who you are						
3. I usually face life as . . .						
A pessimist	1	2	3	4	5	An optimist
4. I feel a sense of control or mastery as I face transitions . . .						
Never	1	2	3	4	5	Always

(continued)

EXHIBIT 7.1. Identify Your Resources for Coping in
Retirement: Sample Questions From the Transition
Guide (TG) *(continued)*

Your supports: What help you have from others						

5. I can count on support from my family . . .						
Never	1	2	3	4	5	Always

6. I can count on support from my friends . . .						
Never	1	2	3	4	5	Always

Your strategies: How you cope						

7. I cope by . . .						
Using few strategies	1	2	3	4	5	Using a range of strategies

8. I cope by . . .						
Seeking advice	1	2	3	4	5	Not seeking advice

Note. For information on the entire Transition Guide, see
http://www.transitionguide.com

8

Create a Lifetime of Possibilities

As I mentioned in chapter 5 of this volume, Dee, the retired State Department official, is now in training to become a motorcycle instructor. Even though few of us will choose motorcycling as our retirement sport, each one of us can retire in a unique way. Your own style, your own way of being in the world reflects what psychologists refer to as "successful" or "positive aging." According to Vaillant, "Positive aging means to love, to work, to learn something we did not know yesterday, and to enjoy the remaining precious moments with loved ones."[1] We can apply that to retirement. Dee is certainly defining her own style, learning something new, and enjoying life. And so can you. It might not be off the beaten path, but it needs to be something that makes you happy and feel that you matter.

MAKE HAPPINESS YOUR PRIORITY

Can you expect to be happy? The answer: Yes, if you live long enough! A major study by sociologist Yang

Yang appeared in the *American Sociological Review*. The data seemed counterintuitive: Yang studied a national sample of 20,000 individuals from ages 18 to 88 and discovered that older individuals were the happiest. If that is really true, why do so many dread aging? Yang also found, however, that baby boomers were not as happy, possibly because their expectations remained high whereas older people may have lowered theirs.[2]

How does this apply to you? John Gottman, a family therapist, contended that happiness depends on the ratio of happy to unhappy events in a person's life. His studies of married couples confirmed that couples see themselves as happy despite unhappy events if the happy events outnumber the unhappy ones.[3]

I asked a group of women living in a retirement community to think about the issues that overwhelmed them. They were unhappy when their children and grandchildren were stressed because they felt unable to control the stressful events. When I asked how many had adult children who had divorced, almost all hands were raised. Those who had less access to their grandchildren were the unhappiest. When I talked individually with these women, they reported experiencing both happy and unhappy events. One woman reported,

> I love living in this community. I feel safe and know if anything happens to me or my husband, we will be cared for. I have made wonderful friends and am having fun. I suffer about my son, who is unhappy, and I miss seeing my grandchildren. But overall, I have to say, I am happy.

So when you are feeling blue, just stop and add up some of the positives in your life. It is hoped that they will outweigh the negatives. If not, try to figure out ways to boost your happiness by building more happy events into your life.

Who will be happy in retirement? At best, we can make only educated guesses. I interviewed Marlene, a retired special education teacher, who was worried about how she would orchestrate her retirement life. At the suggestion of a friend, she went through a difficult application and training process to become a docent at one of the Smithsonian museums. Once accepted, she participated in an ongoing rigorous program requiring study of history, art, and architecture. "I had to fit myself into a new culture of retirement, forcing me to learn new skills and attitudes," she recalled.

After completing the training, Marlene volunteered every Wednesday. When the museum announced it was closing for a 2-year renovation, she was concerned about losing the structure for her week as well as her Wednesday companions. Others felt the same way, so the "Wednesday Group" decided to meet monthly as a way to stay in touch. Marlene also became active in a garden club in her area, serving as its treasurer. She was grateful that her new involvements provided a new routine and structure for her life. Obviously, Marlene had no need to worry. She aced retirement by meeting Cohen's criteria for a successful retirement—engaging in activities that provide a "sense of control"[4] along with enduring relationships and new learnings. She also met Lyubomirsky's criteria of being engaged in a major happiness-boosting activity—showing gratitude.[5] And she met my definition of retirement happiness because she felt she mattered to her Wednesday Group and garden club.

SCREEN FOR MATTERING

Why does mattering matter? Sociologists Leonard Pearlin and Allen LeBlanc studied the consequences of no longer mattering.[6] While engaged in caregiving, people knew they mattered. When their role was over, usually when the care recipient died, they felt diminished, often experiencing a loss of self-esteem, structure, and purpose.

The following examples illustrate how easy it is to lose your sense of mattering. Roz was surprised at the extent of her grief after her husband died. He had been ill for many years. Although she had help 4 hours a day, her life was tied up for 20 hours a day, year after year. Roz assumed she would feel great relief when her husband died. Why, she wondered, was the grieving process so prolonged? The reason was that her entire life changed. Her routines dramatically changed, her role as caregiver terminated, her major relationship was over, and her assumptions about her future were in flux. No wonder her grieving went on and on.

Nora retired from her administrative job in a community theatre at age 60 so that she could realize her dream to move New York, find an agent, and begin auditioning for plays. After a year of pounding the sidewalks with no luck, she returned home. She assumed that her lack of success related to her age. Then she read about two older women who were performing on Broadway. That added insult to injury. Now she could no longer blame her roadblocks solely on her age. Every time she read about another 60-, 70-, or 80-year-old man or woman starring in a Broadway production, she felt sick inside, ashamed of herself for feeling envious, angry at herself for thinking she could do it, and upset that she was being sidelined. Now what would she do? Her loss of mattering was palpable.

Ben, a retired social worker, had some experiences that made him feel marginal, out of touch, and too old. He had been president of a professional association and over the years had remained connected closely with the organization. But for the past few years, he had not been invited to speak or to attend the annual meeting. He assumed that the reason he was no longer invited as a featured speaker related to the organization's need for younger people who were actively working in the field. As an added snub, he discovered that the national meeting would be in the city where he lived, and he felt insulted that no one had invited him to attend the main reception. He concluded that his time was past.

What do Nora, Roz, and Ben do when they no longer matter? Those who are able to forge a new life find that substituting new involvements and activities make the difference. For example, one woman substituted exercise for work. She joined a health club and was a regular in a water aerobics class that met three times a week. She realized that water aerobics was not the same as running a small company, but when she occasionally did not appear, people called her. Then she knew she mattered.

Whether your choice of activity is water aerobics, a book club, a luncheon group, a part-time job, or a volunteer job does not matter—the specifics are irrelevant. What matters is that you matter to yourself, to others, and to the community at large. A happy retirement depends heavily on these feelings. Remember, if your life is not going the way you want it today, it is critical to turn your life around because the consequences of not mattering can lead to sadness and even depression.

NOT MATTERING—A NONEVENT

The flip side of mattering is not mattering, and sometimes it happens despite our best efforts. If you expect to be appreciated and for some reason you are ignored or sidelined, you are experiencing what I call a *nonevent*, meaning that the event you expected did not occur. Ben expected to remain connected to his professional association, and Roz did not realize how empty she would feel when she no longer had a caregiver role. Nonevents are hidden, often not discussed, and can lead to unsettled feelings.

In the numerous studies of nonevents that I conducted with students at the University of Maryland and with Susan Robinson of the American Council on Education, it became clear that coping with nonevents demands special strategies. Because nonevents are often unrecognized, it is difficult to rehearse for them. We found that people go through a process, not necessarily in the same order, of acknowledging, grieving, refocusing, and reshaping their lost dreams.[7]

At some point, you need to acknowledge your nonevent and give it a name. This has the double effect of diluting its power and of helping you take control of the situation. The question of how to acknowledge your nonevents to others is very important. People do not usually go around saying, "Let me tell you about my retirement nonevent—the job offer that never came." Unless you let others know you are experiencing a painful nonevent, they will not know how to comfort you or even that you need comforting. So telling a story that makes your pain explicit can help mobilize others to help you.

After acknowledging your nonevent, you may need to grieve. It is easy to recognize the grief that accompanies the death of a significant person in one's life. But it's also important to deal with your grief over what did not happen—a book that was never published, a job that was not offered, a relationship that never materialized, or a retirement that did not occur. Make the grief visible to others so they can step up to the plate to give you needed support. If you don't let them know, there will be no wakes, no chicken soup. The sadness will intensify.

The next part of the process can be difficult: letting go of old expectations and reframing the nonevent. People have difficulty changing their perceptions of themselves and the world, but shifting focus is necessary. Then, reshape new goals with an eye to the future, forcefully identifying a new dream or a new vision.

Reshaping includes taking stock and transforming the old dream by imagining another, more possible future. Harry and Kim decided they had to keep working, but they moved into a nearby retirement community. They gave up their dream of a carefree retirement and settled for something more realistic. They did it, but it was not easy.

I am often asked, "How long will this dream reshaping process take?" It would be great to be able to provide a definitive answer, but the amount of time depends on the person, the nature of the nonevent, and the supports he or she has. Taking stock, regaining control, transforming the dream—these are critical. Should Nora give up the dream of the theater entirely and put the dream on hold? Or should she develop an entirely new dream?

If you have decided it is time to reshape your dream, then think of alternative scenarios. Find new outlets—ones that will make you feel good about yourself and productive, as if what you are doing is important.

CONTINUE LEARNING

We are constantly in transition—exiting from one job, relationship, career, or location and trying to figure out what's next. To help in the quest, the Atlantic Philanthropies announced special demonstration grants to the American Association of Community Colleges to promote civic engagement and lifelong learning. Ten community colleges will design model programs to engage boomers in encore careers. Training will include skills in tutoring low-income children, environmental jobs such as restoring wetlands, health care, entrepreneurship, personal finance, technology, literacy, nursing, and other endeavors. These programs will attract retirees and provide training for their encore volunteer or paid careers.

In a study completed many years ago by the College Board, the authors identified a universal need to use education as a way to deal with inevitable personal and work transitions.[8] A recent MetLife Foundation/ American Council on Education study found that education was the link for individuals to figure out their futures. The study highlighted an overlooked point:

> Baby boomers . . . have also experienced the "largest wage inequality of any cohort to date." . . . Between 1980 and 2000, the share of aggregate income of the wealthiest one-fifth of boomer households increased, while those in the bottom four-fifths diminished."[9]

This is a startling figure because so much of the literature promotes the notion of the wealthy boomer. But if many boomers are at the bottom economically, many writers assume that the best way they can increase their incomes is through education.[10]

If you want to add zest to your life, the best place to start is by learning something new. And once you start, you never know where it might take you. Jay, a retired educational administrator, started spending time in the local library. He loved reading books and spent hours in the library reading the classics he never had time to read as a younger man. After a while, he became aware of homeless people hanging out in the lobby of the library or using the bathrooms. He began to talk to some of the regulars and found that many were very industrious, but because of the state of the economy, they were unable to make a decent living. He started to help them find jobs. This is an example of how one activity—reading the classics—led to working on a modern-day problem.

Learning will help you explore possibilities that will take into account your need to redefine your identity, deepen your relationships, and regain a sense of purpose. There are many places where you can study, such as Elderhostel programs, community centers, religious institutions, free-standing organizations, colleges and universities that offer free classes for seniors as well as credit courses, and much more. I attended an awards celebration for retired men and women attending an art education center. They were engaged in their pursuit of art—painting, sculpting, printmaking, and jewelry making—and participating in a community of like-minded individuals. Above all, they were deeply engaged in life.

CONCLUSION

To be happy, you need perspective and skill: perspective that retirement is an evolution of your career development and that you must be prepared for surprises;

skill in finding a connector who can link you with opportunities that make you feel you matter. In addition, you need to build those elusive qualities of resilience and patience. To matter, you need to acknowledge the ways in which you do not matter and move on to create new possibilities.

In his book *Aging Well: Surprising Guideposts to a Happier Life*, Vaillant wrote,

> Successful aging means giving to others joyously whenever one is able, receiving from others gratefully whenever one needs it, and being greedy enough to develop one's own self in between. Such balance comes . . . from employing elegant unconscious coping mechanisms that make lemonade out of lemons.[11]

If this were a test of retirement—not just aging—would you pass it?

IT'S YOUR TURN: ARE YOU READY FOR WHAT'S NEXT?

1. Think About Your Life and Figure Out Your Path

If you are retired, are you on the path you want to be on? Are you focusing on your passion? Are you grabbing onto happenstance? Julie, a retired beautician, heard someone talk at a meeting about a new national endeavor that provides community support for those living in a prescribed geographic area. This is an effort to help people remain in their own homes but with available supports like transportation, caregiving, and so on.

She followed up by calling the speaker about the project. Now she's part of the planning group that will implement the project in her neighborhood. Three months before, she had been floundering. Today, she is energized and excited.

If you are considering retirement, this might be the time to figure out which path would be best for you, now and for the foreseeable future. Are you already on a path you like? Should you stay there or make a change? To help you find some answers to these questions, reflect on the pros and cons of several paths based on your psychological portfolio. Take this opportunity to examine your current and future life and to make informed decisions about "getting a life"— or, more specifically, "getting a new life."

2. Make Sure You Matter

Make a list of places, people, and activities that make you feel you matter. Consider the following questions:

- Have you made a plan for substitute communities of friends and acquaintances after leaving work?
- Have you imagined what you will do to excite and energize you after work?

Afterword

This book has focused on you as an individual—what you can do to make your retirement rewarding and meaningful. The emphasis thus far has been on ways to tap into your own creativity and perspectives on how you can make your mark.

Now for the caveat: We do not live as individual stars. We are part of a galaxy. Ask yourself, "Am I living in a community that provides the freedom and support needed as I, and others, transition into and out of retirement, work, and family? If not, how can I help create such a community?" I propose that you consider being part of a small solution—a program that rejuvenates and jump-starts opportunities for prospective and current retirees.

A Community Proposal— An Internship Program for Retirees

Members of each path discussed in chapter 5 of this volume—Continuer, Adventurer, Searcher, Easy Glider,

Involved Spectator, and Retreater—will eventually start a search for what's next as they try to find a niche. For example, I knew a retired teacher who moved to Washington State expecting to be welcomed with open arms and immediately involved in meaningful work. It has not happened the way she anticipated, and she is searching for her niche. Another Searcher I met was the senior editor of a national newspaper who planned to retire soon. He had no idea what he wanted to do or what would be available to him. Searchers run the entire spectrum from blue collar to white collar, rich to poor, young to old. One Adventurer who is constantly on the move, hiking to exotic places, is now ready to slow down. She is beginning to search for new avenues—still exciting—but less stressful.

Searchers could benefit from a structure that would help them figure out what's next, and because we will all be Searchers at some time, I suggest a possible solution: Establish an Explorers Club, a support group for Searchers that meets regularly to discuss the choices they are facing and coordinates internships in the community. Each Searcher would be assigned to a mentor who would place the Searcher as an intern in an organization congruent with the searcher's interests and needs. For example, a building contractor who is interested in learning about fundraising might be placed in a nonprofit organization to assist the professional fundraiser. He is also interested in plants, so his second internship might be at a botanical garden. A legal secretary who has always had a desire to paint could be placed as an intern with one of the many artists in her community. The possibilities are endless for this project, and it would illustrate that your community cares enough to make retirees know they matter.

Making such a program happen takes a group of leaders with energy and initiative. This group would begin by locating an organization that would sponsor such a program, developing a marketing plan that would reach Searchers, and identifying organizations in the community that would provide the internships. Launching a community program would be a win–win situation: The community will win; retirees will win.

BUILDING A CARING COMMUNITY FOR ALL

Individuals are highly variable in their development and become increasingly so as they grow older, but it is still possible to identify some universal themes that cut across race, gender, ethnicity, age, and social class. Even as people change careers, goals, partners, and cities, the themes of identity, intimacy, competency, and mattering crop up. I am struck by the similarity between my son Mark, when he was 18, and my friend Tresa, when she was 75. Though of different ages and dealing with different life decisions, they had much in common.

Mark was perplexed about his future when he graduated from high school. He had been a football star. Who was he now that he'd hung up that uniform? Would he have the competency to deal with next steps? Would he make new friends who would be as close as his buddies in the locker room? Would anything in life make him feel he still mattered as much as when the cheerleaders sang his praises?

Tresa had just become a widow after 50 years of marriage. She wondered who she would be without her husband. Would she have the competency to deal with life alone, especially because she had a chronic health problem? Would she still be included in her social group now that she was alone?

Tresa and Mark were very different in every respect but one: their uncertainty about the universal themes of identity, intimacy, competency, and mattering. They were both in limbo, experiencing major transitions and facing many of the same underlying questions. They were unsure of who they would become and whether or not they had the competency to deal with the ambiguities ahead. In a caring community, people of all ages and backgrounds would have opportunities to relate around these universal issues, especially the need to matter.

TOGETHER INTO THE UNKNOWN

I recently saw a collection of maps of the ancient world. Skillful and proud of their accomplishments as the old cartographers must have been, they had no way of knowing that they had left out whole countries, even whole continents. It struck me that these maps might be a good metaphor for our retirement years. We start out from the work world we have known and travel into uncharted territory—although we need not fear falling off the end of the earth. There might be a similarity between the mapmakers' unsure grasp of reality and that of people in transition—though both need to carry on even when they are off track. The mapmaker corrects the map when faced with reality; those in transition are constantly pursuing one course of action that later might need modification depending on a new reality.

So whether we follow the current or ply our rudder to choose a course, we are sure to reach a place where we can begin to fashion a new world for ourselves. There we can be happy, content, and fulfilled, perhaps even more than we were in the old world of our previous lives.

Here's wishing you wind in your sails. And remember, mattering matters.

Notes

INTRODUCTION

1. Robinson, S. P., & Lakin, M. B. (2007). *Framing new terrain: Older adults & higher education.* Washington, DC: American Council on Education, p. 4.
2. Heimer, M., & Bellstrom, K. (2006, March 15). Retire happy. *SmartMoney.* Retrieved August 25, 2008, from http://www.smartmoney.com/cover/index.cfm?Story=april2006&hpadref=1
3. Cohen, G. (2008, March 31). *Creativity and psychological growth with aging: Positive changes that occur because of aging, not despite aging.* Speech presented at the Cosmos Club, Washington, DC.
4. Cohen, G. D. (2005). *The mature mind: The positive power of the aging brain.* New York: Basic Books. See pp. xvii, 126.
5. Freedman, M. (1999). *Prime time: How baby boomers will revolutionize retirement and transform America.* New York: Public Affairs, p. viii.
6. Mintel International Group. (2006, May). *Retire-mentality—U.S.* Available at http://oxygen.mintel.com/sinatra/reports/display/id=180079/display/id=180079
7. Reinink, A. (2006, November 20). Baby boomers show this isn't your father's retirement. *Sarasota Herald-Tribune,* p. 5B.

8. Mintel International Group. (2006, May). *Retire-mentality—U.S.* Available at http://oxygen.mintel.com/sinatra/reports/display/id=180079/display/id=180079

9. Smith, L. (2006, October 15). Boom time: The generation that wrote its own rules now looks to redefine the concept of aging. *Baltimore Sun,* Modern Life, Section N, p. 1.

10. Rubin, L. B. (2007). *60 on up: The truth about aging in America.* Boston, MA: Beacon Press, p. 10.

11. Schlossberg, N. K. (2004). *Retire smart, retire happy: Finding your true path in life.* Washington, DC: American Psychological Association.

12. Rosenberg, M. (n.d.) *Self-concept and psychological well-being: Mattering and verdicality.* Unpublished manuscript.

13. Rosenberg, M., & McCullough, B. C. (1981). Mattering: Inferred significance to parents and mental health among adolescents. In R. Simmons (Ed.), *Research in community and mental health* (Vol. 2, pp. 163–182). Greenwich, CT: JAI Press, pp. 179–180.

14. Rosenberg, M. (n.d.). *Self-concept and psychological well-being: Mattering and veridicality.* Unpublished manuscript. See pp. 1–2.

15. Schlossberg, N. K., Lynch, A. Q., & Chickering, A. W. (1989). *Improving higher education environments for adults: Responsive programs and services from entry to departure.* San Francisco: Jossey-Bass.

16. Rosenberg, F. (1992). *Wives of first term soldiers: An analysis of survey results* (Publication No. WRAIR/TR-94-0014). Washington, DC: Walter Reed Army Institute of Research.

17. Rosenberg, F. (1993). *Survey of Army families 1991: A multivariate analysis.* Washington, DC: Walter Reed Army Institute of Research, Uniformed Services University of the Health Sciences.

CHAPTER 1. THE KEY TO A HAPPY RETIREMENT

1. Rosenberg, M., & McCullough, B. C. (1981). Mattering: Inferred significance to parents and mental health among adolescents. In R. Simmons (Ed.), *Research in community and mental health* (Vol. 2, pp. 163–182). Greenwich, CT: JAI Press.

2. Schlossberg, N. K., Lassalle, A., & Golec, R. (1998). *The Mattering Scales for adult students in higher education*. Washington, DC: Center for Adult Learning, American Council on Education.

3. Rosenberg, M., & McCullough, B. C. (1981). Mattering: Inferred significance to parents and mental health among adolescents. In R. Simmons (Ed.), *Research in community and mental health* (Vol. 2, pp. 163–182). Greenwich, CT: JAI Press.

4. Weiss, R. S. (2005). *The experience of retirement*. Ithaca, NY, and London: Cornell University Press, pp. 3–5.

5. Brooks, D. (2006, March 19). Run Baruck, run. *New York Times*, p. 12.

6. Putnam, R. D. (2000). *Bowling alone: The collapse and revival of American community*. New York: Simon & Schuster.

7. Freedman, M. (2007). *Encore: Finding work that matters in the second half of life*. New York: Perseus Publishing, p. vii.

8. Dutton, T. (2005, July 3). What's at stake in a quest to matter. *Sarasota Herald-Tribune*, "Perspectives" section, pp. 1, 6.

9. Rosenberg, M. (n.d.) *Self-concept and psychological well-being: Mattering and verdicality*. Unpublished manuscript.

10. Schooler, C., & Mulatu, M. S. (2001). The reciprocal effects of leisure time activities and intellectual functioning in older people: A longitudinal analysis. *Psychology and Aging, 16*(3), 466–482.

11. Kahn, R. L. (2004, March 20). *Successful aging: Myth or reality?* 2004 Winkelman Lecture, School of Social Work, University of Michigan, Ann Arbor.

12. Yeoman, B. (2006, March–April). Rethinking the commune. *AARP the Magazine,* pp. 88–97.

13. Gilbert, D. (2006). *Stumbling on happiness.* New York: Knopf, pp. 16–17.

14. Seligman, M. E. P. (2002). *Authentic happiness: Using the new positive psychology to realize your potential for lasting fulfillment.* New York: Free Press, p. 45.

15. Stallone, D. D., & Stunkard, A. J. (1991). The regulation of body weight: Evidence and clinical implications. *Annals of Behavioral Medicine, 3,* 220–230.

16. Lyubomirsky, S. (2007). *The how of happiness: A scientific approach to getting the life you want.* New York: Penguin Press.

17. Gilbert, D. (2006). *Stumbling on happiness.* New York: Knopf, p. 30.

18. Diener, E. (2008, September 1). Personal communication.

19. Quoted in Hagedorn, H. (1948). *Prophet in the wilderness: The story of Albert Schweitzer.* New York: Macmillan, p. 188.

20. Cohen, G. D. (2005). *The mature mind: The positive power of the aging brain.* New York: Basic Books, p. xvii.

21. Brown, C. (2004, May). The (scientific) pursuit of happiness. *Smithsonian Magazine,* pp. 102–108, pp. 102–103.

22. Quoted in Wallace, B. A., & Shapiro, S. L. (2006, October). Mental balance and well-being: Building bridges between Buddhism and Western psychology. *American Psychologist, 61,* 690–701, p. 691.

23. Gilbert, D. (2006). *Stumbling on happiness.* New York: Knopf, p. 238.

24. Rosenberg, M. (n.d.). *Self-concept and psychological well-being: Mattering and veridicality.* Unpublished manuscript.

25. Gilbert, D. (2006). *Stumbling on happiness.* New York: Knopf, p. 34.

Chapter 2. Check Your Psychological Portfolio

1. WGBH Boston (Producer), Comiskey, B. (Director), & Schlossberg, N. K. (Writer). (2008). *Retire smart, retire happy* [DVD]. United States: PBS.

2. Alumnae Association of Barnard College, Research Committee of Project Continuum. (2004, September). *Barnard women in transition: How alumnae are coping with work and retirement*. New York: Author.

3. Levinson, D. J. (1978). *The seasons of a man's life*. New York: Knopf.

4. Josselson, R. (1996). *Revising herself: The story of women's identity from college to midlife*. New York: Oxford University Press, p. 29.

5. Josselson, R. (1987). *Finding herself: Pathways to identity development in women*. San Francisco: Jossey-Bass, p. 256.

6. Josselson, R. (1996). *Revising herself: The story of women's identity from college to midlife*. New York: Oxford University Press, p. 27.

7. Josselson, R. (1987). *Finding herself: Pathways to identity development in women*. San Francisco: Jossey-Bass.

8. Maddi, S. R., & Khoshaba, D. M. (2005). *Resilience at work: How to succeed no matter what life throws at you*. Washington, DC: AMACOM, p. 94

9. Reyes, K. W. (2006, November–December). The movers and the stayers: A new AARP study reveals why there's still no place like home. *AARP Magazine*, p. 94.

10. McPherson, M., Smith, L. L., & Brashear, M. E. (2006, June). Social isolation in America: Changes in core discussion networks over two decades. *American Sociological Review, 71*, 353–375.

11. Putnam, R. D. (2000). *Bowling alone: The collapse and revival of American community*. New York: Simon & Schuster. See discussion in chapter 1, this volume.

12. Cohen, G. D. (2005). *The mature mind: The positive power of the aging brain*. New York: Basic Books, pp. xvii, 126.

13. Moen, P. (2003). *It's about time: Couples and careers*. Ithaca, NY, and London: ILR Press and Cornell University Press.

14. Moen, P., & Fields, V. (2002). Midcourse in the United States: Does unpaid community participation replace paid work? *Aging International, 27*(3), 21–48.

15. WGBH Boston (Producer), Comiskey, B. (Director), & Schlossberg, N. K. (Writer). (2008). *Retire smart, retire happy* [DVD]. United States: PBS.

16. Weiss, R. S. (2005). *The experience of retirement*. Ithaca, NY, and London: Cornell University Press, p. 103.

17. Badalato, W. (Executive Producer), Begley, L. (Writer), Payne, A. (Writer/Director), & Taylor, J. (Writer). (2002). *About Schmidt* [Motion picture]. United States: New Line Cinema.

18. Freedman, M. (1999). *Prime time: How baby boomers will revolutionize retirement and transform America*. New York: Public Affairs, p. viii.

19. Freedman, M. (1999). *Prime time: How baby boomers will revolutionize retirement and transform America*. New York: Public Affairs, p. viii.

20. Freedman, M. (2007). *Encore: Finding work that matters in the second half of life*. New York: Perseus Publishing, p. vii.

CHAPTER 3. REVITALIZE YOUR IDENTITY

1. Vaillant, G. E. (2002). *Aging well: Surprising guideposts to a happier life*. New York: Little, Brown.

2. Costa, P. T., & McCrae, R. R. (1989). Personality continuity and the changes of adult life. In M. Storandt & G. R. VandenBos (Eds.), *The adult years: Continuity*

and change (pp. 45–77). Washington, DC: American Psychological Association.

3. Vaillant, G. E. (2002). *Aging well: Surprising guideposts to a happier life*. New York: Little, Brown, pp. 284–285.

4. McAdams, D. P. (2006). *The redemptive self: Stories Americans live by*. New York: Oxford University Press, p. 84.

5. McAdams, D. P. (2008, March 26). Personal communication.

6. Hopcke, R. H. (1997). *There are no accidents: Synchronicity and the stories of our lives*. New York: Riverhead Books.

7. Krumboltz, J. D., & Levin, A. S. (2004). *Luck is no accident: Making the most of happenstance in your life and career*. Atascadero, CA: Impact.

8. Brim, G. (1992). *Ambition: How we manage success and failure throughout our lives*. New York: Basic Books.

9. Costa, P. T., & McCrae, R. R. (1989). Personality continuity and the changes of adult life. In M. Storandt & G. R. VandenBos (Eds.), *The adult years: Continuity and change* (pp. 45–77). Washington, DC: American Psychological Association.

10. Maddi, S. R. (2002). The story of hardiness: Twenty years of theorizing, research, and practice. *Consulting Psychology Journal, 54,* 173–185, p. 177.

11. American Psychological Association. (2004). *The road to resilience*. Copyright 2004 by the American Psychological Association. Retrieved August 25, 2008, from http://www.apahelpcenter.org/featuredtopics/feature.php?id=6&ch=4

12. Cooperrider, D. L., & Whitney, D. (2005). *Appreciative Inquiry: A positive revolution in change*. San Francisco: Berrett-Koehler.

CHAPTER 4. REVITALIZE YOUR RELATIONSHIPS

1. Moen, P., & Fields, V. (2002). Midcourse in the United States: Does unpaid community participation replace paid work? *Aging International, 27*(3), 21–48.
2. Gladwell, M. (2000). *The tipping point: How little things can make a big difference*. New York: Little, Brown. See p. 38.
3. Quoted in Gladwell, M. (2000). *The tipping point: How little things can make a big difference*. New York: Little, Brown, p. 54.
4. Savickes, M. (2006). Personal communication.
5. Bratter, B., & Dennis, H. (2008). *Project renewment: The first retirement model for career women*. New York: Simon & Schuster.
6. McElroy, S. (2006, October 11). Lift every over-50 voice and sing, ladies, sing. *New York Times*, p. B3.
7. MetLife Mature Market Institute, AARP Health Care Options, & Matthew Greenwald and Associates. (2004). *The future of retirement living*. Westport, CT: Authors.
8. Kahn, R. L. (2004, March 20). *Successful aging: Myth or reality?* 2004 Winkelman Lecture, School of Social Work, University of Michigan, Ann Arbor.
9. Bernhard, W. (2008, March). Women's creative aging. *Clio's Psyche, 14*(4), 120–127.
10. Bernhard, W. (2008, April). Personal communication.
11. Furlong, M. S. (2007). *Turning silver into gold: How to profit in the new boomer marketplace*. Upper Saddle River, NJ: FT Press.
12. Taylor, S. E. (2002). *The tending instinct: Women, men, and the biology of our relationships*. New York: Times Books, Henry Holt.
13. Rubin, L. B. (1985). *Just friends: The role of friendship in our lives*. New York: Harper & Row, p. 13.
14. Segal, A. (2006). *Battered heart*. Sarasota, FL: Peppertree Press.

15. Cohen, G. D. (2005). *The mature mind: The positive power of the aging brain.* New York: Basic Books, pp. xvii, 126.

CHAPTER 5. REVITALIZE YOUR PURPOSE

1. Cohen, G. D. (2000). *The creative age: Awakening human potential in the second half of life.* New York: HarperCollins.
2. AARP. (2003). *Staying ahead of the curve 2003: The AARP working in retirement study* [Executive summary]. Washington, DC: Author.
3. Furlong, M. S. (2007). *Turning silver into gold: How to profit in the new boomer marketplace.* Upper Saddle River, NJ: FT Press.
4. Freedman, M. (2007). *Encore: Finding work that matters in the second half of life.* New York: Perseus Publishing.
5. Heimer, M., & Bellstrom, K. (2006, March 15). Retire happy. *SmartMoney.* Retrieved August 25, 2008, from http://www.smartmoney.com/cover/index.cfm?Story= april2006&hpadref=1
6. McAdams, D. P., Hart, H. M., & Maruna, S. (1998). The anatomy of generativity. In D. P. McAdams & E. de St. Aubin (Eds.), *Generativity and adult development: How and why we care for the next generation* (pp. 7–44). Washington, DC: American Psychological Association, p. 10.
7. McAdams, D. P., Hart, H. M., & Maruna, S. (1998). The anatomy of generativity. In D. P. McAdams & E. de St. Aubin (Eds.), *Generativity and adult development: How and why we care for the next generation* (pp. 7–44). Washington, DC: American Psychological Association, p. 13.
8. Erikson, E. H., Erikson, J. M., & Kivnick, H. Q. (1987). *Vital involvement in old age.* New York: Norton.

9. Taylor, S. E. (2002). *The tending instinct: Women, men, and the biology of our relationships*. New York: Times Books, Henry Holt & Co, p. 3.

10. McAdams, D. P., & de St. Aubin, E. (1998). *Generativity and adult development: How and why we care for the next generation*. Washington, DC: American Psychological Association.

11. WGBH Boston (Producer), Comiskey, B. (Director), & Schlossberg, N. K. (Writer). (2008). *Retire smart, retire happy* [DVD]. United States: PBS.

12. WGBH Boston (Producer), Comiskey, B. (Director), & Schlossberg, N. K. (Writer). (2008). *Retire smart, retire happy* [DVD]. United States: PBS.

13. Casper, L. M., & Bryson, K. R. (1998, March). *Co-resident grandparents and their grandchildren: Grandparent maintained families* (Population Division Working Paper No. 26). Washington, DC: U.S. Census Bureau, Population Division.

14. Vaillant, G. E. (2002). *Aging well: Surprising guideposts to a happier life*. New York: Little, Brown, p. 229.

15. Furlong, M. S. (2007). *Turning silver into gold: How to profit in the new boomer marketplace*. Upper Saddle River, NJ: FT Press, p. 45.

16. Schlossberg, N. K. (2004). *Retire smart, retire happy: Finding your true path in life*. Washington, DC: American Psychological Association.

17. Schlossberg, N. K. (2004). *Retire smart, retire happy: Finding your true path in life*. Washington, DC: American Psychological Association.

18. Friedan, B. (1993). *The fountain of age*. New York: Simon & Schuster.

19. Billig, N. (1987). *To be old and sad: Understanding depression in the elderly*. Lanham, MD: Lexington Books.

Chapter 6. It's About You: Design Your Own Psychological Portfolio

1. Gilbert, D. (2006). *Stumbling on happiness.* New York: Knopf.
2. Gilbert, D. (2006). *Stumbling on happiness.* New York: Knopf.
3. Church, G. J. (1998, September 7). Unmasking age bias. *Time.* Retrieved August 25, 2008, from http://www.time.com/time/magazine/article/0,9171,989026,00.html
4. Neugarten, B. (1977). Adaptation and the life cycle. In N. K. Schlossberg & A. D. Entine (Eds.), *Counseling adults* (pp. 34–36). Monterey, CA: Brooks/Cole.
5. Gilbert, D. (2006). *Stumbling on happiness.* New York: Knopf.
6. SCOPE. (2006). *SCOPE 2006 annual report.* Available from SCOPE, 1226 N. Tamiami Trail, Suite 202, Sarasota, FL 34236.

Chapter 7. Three Guidelines for a Better Retirement

1. Schlossberg, N. K. (2008). *Overwhelmed: Coping with life's ups and downs* (2nd ed.). Lanham, MD: Evans.
2. Schlossberg, N. K. (2008). *Overwhelmed: Coping with life's ups and downs* (2nd ed.). Latham, MD: Evans, p. 78.
3. Rubin, L. B. (2006, Fall). What am I going to do with the rest of my life? *Dissent,* pp. 88–94, pp. 93–94.
4. Ardelt, M. (2003). Empirical assessment of a three-dimensional wisdom scale. *Research on Aging, 25*(3), 275–324.
5. Gladwell, M. (2005). *Blink: The power of thinking without thinking.* New York: Little, Brown, p. 23.

6. Rubin, L. B. (2007). *60 on up: The truth about aging in America.* Boston: Beacon Press.

7. WGBH Boston (Producer), Comiskey, B. (Director), & Schlossberg, N. K. (Writer). (2008). *Retire smart, retire happy* [DVD]. United States: PBS.

8. Lazarus, R. S. (1991). *Emotion and adaptation.* New York: Oxford University Press, p. 16.

9. Lazarus, R., & Folkman, S. (1984). *Stress, appraisal, and coping.* New York: Springer Publishing Company.

10. Fredrickson, B. L., Tugade, M. M., Waugh, C. E., & Larkin, G. R. (2003). What good are positive emotions in crises? A prospective study of resilience and emotions following the terrorist attacks on the United States on September 11th, 2001. *Journal of Personality and Social Psychology, 84*(2), 365–376, p. 367.

11. Bateson, M. C. (1989). *Composing a life.* New York: Atlantic Monthly Press, pp. 6–7.

12. Caplin, L., Colpaert, C., & Matz, Z. (Producers); Sacks, R. (Writer); & Ireland, D. (Director). (2005). *Mrs. Palfrey at the Claremont* [Motion picture]. England: Claremont Films. Note that Ruth used the name "Sacks" in her screenwriting credit but is known by all her friends as Ruth Caplin.

CHAPTER 8. CREATE A LIFETIME OF POSSIBILITIES

1. Vaillant, G. E. (2002). *Aging well: Surprising guideposts to a happier life.* New York: Little, Brown, p. 16.

2. Yang, Y. (2008). Social inequalities in happiness in the United States, 1972 to 2004: An age-period-cohort analysis. *American Sociological Review, 73*(2), 204–226.

3. Gottman discussed in Vedantam, S. (2007, October 1). Is great happiness too much of a good thing? *Washington Post,* p. A9.

4. Cohen, G. D. (2005). *The mature mind: The positive power of the aging brain.* New York: Basic Books, pp. xvii, 126.

5. Lyubomirsky, S. (2007). *The how of happiness: A scientific approach to getting the life you want*. New York: Penguin Press, p. 89.

6. Pearlin, L. I., & LeBlanc, A. J. (2001). Bereavement and the loss of mattering. In T. J. Owens & S. Stryker (Eds.), *Extending self-esteem theory and research: Sociological and psychological currents* (pp. 285–300). New York: Cambridge University Press.

7. Schlossberg, N. K., & Robinson, S. P. (1996). *Going to Plan B: How you can cope, regroup, and start your life on a new path*. New York: Simon & Schuster.

8. Aslanian, C. B., & Brickell, H. N. (1980). *Americans in transition: Life change and reasons for adult learning*. New York: College Entrance Examination Board.

9. Robinson, S. P., & Lakin, M. B. (2007, October). *Framing new terrain: Older adults and higher education*. Washington, DC: American Council on Education.

10. Robinson, S. P., & Lakin, M. B. (2007, October). *Framing new terrain: Older adults and higher education*. Washington, DC: American Council on Education, p. 11.

11. Vaillant, G. E. (2002). *Aging well: Surprising guideposts to a happier life*. New York: Little, Brown, p. 61.

Index

About the Author

Nancy K. Schlossberg, EdD, counseling psychologist, is the author of nine books, including *Retire Smart, Retire Happy* and *Overwhelmed: Coping With Life's Ups and Downs*, and is coauthor of *Going to Plan B: How You Can Cope, Regroup, and Start Your Life on a New Path.* She is copresident of TransitionWorks, a consulting firm; professor emerita at the College of Education, University of Maryland, College Park; and past president of the National Career Development Association. She is a fellow in three divisions of the American Psychological Association and in the National Career Development Association and has been a frequent guest on radio and TV programs. Dr. Schlossberg's work was showcased on the front page of *USA Today* and has been quoted in the *New York Times*, the *St. Petersburg Times*, *The Wall Street Journal*, *Reader's Digest*, and Cleveland's *The Plain Dealer*. She and her book *Retire Smart, Retire Happy: Finding Your True Path in Life* were the focus of a 90-minute PBS special that is available on DVD.